family
italian

family
italian

Hearty recipes for everyday cooking

John Lanzafame

MURDOCH BOOKS

contents

mamma mia!

Great food is my parents' passion. They were both born in southern Italy — this is where they met and married, too. Growing up they didn't have a lot of money but this meant that nothing was ever wasted: meat would be salted and hung to dry so it would last for a year, ripe fruit and vegetables would be pickled and eaten throughout the off-season, and bread was baked in a communal town oven every Saturday because it was too expensive to run a wood-fired oven at home.

They eventually immigrated to Australia and shortly after my brother Tony and I were born. We grew up surrounded by an enormous variety of Italian food, and eating it was always special — the family would gather together every single night for dinner. This ritual instilled in me a real sense of the importance of family.

Mum never cooked the same meal twice. As a kid, there was something different to enjoy every day. My mum's creativity introduced me to a whole array of beautiful Italian food. When we were sick, Mum would know what soup to make so we'd feel better; if we did something special, Mum would prepare our favourite meal; every kind of occasion was made more colourful with food.

This book was incredibly important for me to write. It's a collection of my mum's recipes; simple, gutsy and phenomenal meals that she's cooked for many, many years. I'm a firm believer in recording yesterday's recipes, otherwise they'll be lost forever. Inside these pages I've taken Mum's traditional recipes and made them slightly more modern, although they're still nourishing, seasonal, perfect for grazing and all about family.

Mum has always supported me in my endeavours, and this is my acknowledgement to her for being such a major influence in my life and career. As for Dad, at 83, he's still enjoying Mum's cooking, and I've never heard him complain once.

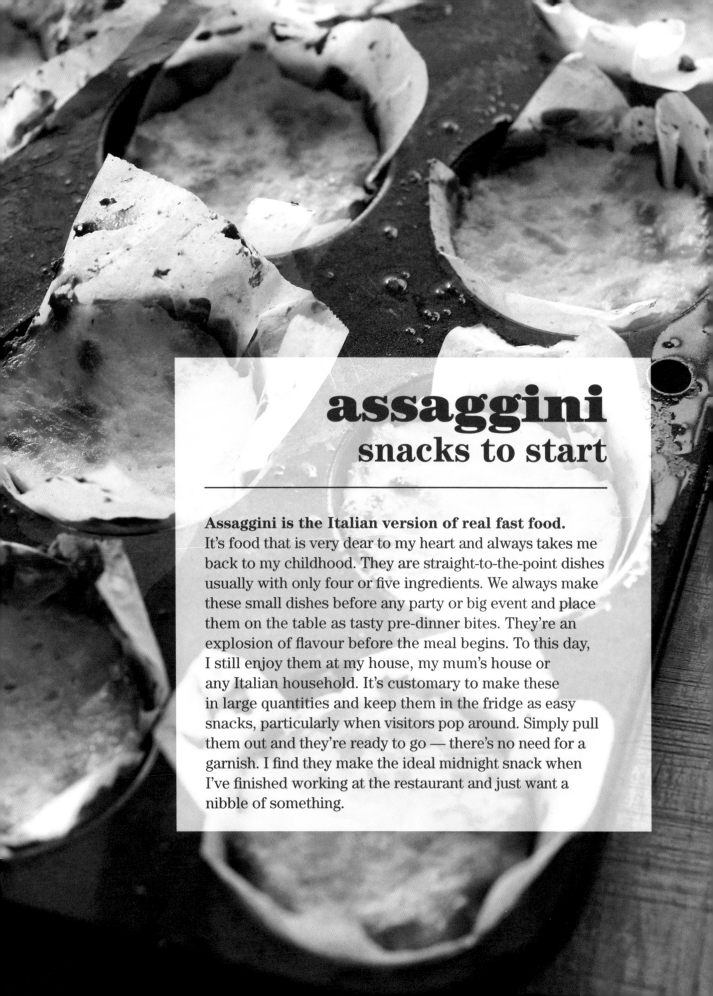

assaggini
snacks to start

Assaggini is the Italian version of real fast food.
It's food that is very dear to my heart and always takes me
back to my childhood. They are straight-to-the-point dishes
usually with only four or five ingredients. We always make
these small dishes before any party or big event and place
them on the table as tasty pre-dinner bites. They're an
explosion of flavour before the meal begins. To this day,
I still enjoy them at my house, my mum's house or
any Italian household. It's customary to make these
in large quantities and keep them in the fridge as easy
snacks, particularly when visitors pop around. Simply pull
them out and they're ready to go — there's no need for a
garnish. I find they make the ideal midnight snack when
I've finished working at the restaurant and just want a
nibble of something.

crochette di prosciutto

prosciutto croquettes

serves 6

50 g (1¾ oz) peeled desiree potato
(about 1 small potato)
2 tablespoons olive oil,
plus extra for deep-frying
2 garlic cloves, sliced
70 g (2½ oz) prosciutto,
finely chopped
40 g (1½ oz) butter
50 g (1¾ oz/⅓ cup) plain
(all-purpose) flour
2 egg yolks

Place the potato in a saucepan of cold, lightly salted water and bring to the boil. Cook until tender. Drain, then mash until smooth and set aside.

Heat the oil in a frying pan over low heat. Add the garlic and stir for 2 minutes or until golden. Add the prosciutto and cook for 1–2 minutes or until heated through but not browned. Add the mashed potato, season to taste with sea salt and freshly ground black pepper and combine well. Remove from the heat and set aside.

Place the butter, 90 ml (3 fl oz) cold water and a pinch of salt in a small heavy-based saucepan and bring to a simmer. Add the flour and mix thoroughly with a wooden spoon until the mixture is smooth and begins to come away from the sides of the pan. Remove from the heat and beat in the egg yolks. Add the prosciutto mixture and combine well. Allow to cool slightly.

Shape tablespoons of mixture into croquettes and place on a baking tray lined with baking paper.

Heat the extra oil in a large deep saucepan or deep-fryer to 160°C (315°F) or until a cube of bread dropped into the oil browns in 30 seconds. Deep-fry the croquettes, in batches, until golden all over. Remove using tongs, drain on absorbent paper and serve warm.

olive marinate con agrumi
citrus-marinated olives

fills one 500 ml (17 fl oz/2 cup) capacity jar

Using a small sharp knife or vegetable peeler, remove one-quarter of the peel from the lemon and blood orange and all of the peel from the orange, then remove any bitter white pith from the peel. Set aside.

Segment the lemon and both oranges, making sure there are no seeds or pith. Set aside.

Heat the oil in a small saucepan over low heat. Add the peppercorns and garlic and cook for 2 minutes or until the garlic just softens. Add the herbs and cook for another 2 minutes, then remove from the heat. Add the citrus peel, combine well and stand until cool.

Transfer the oil mixture to a bowl, add the olives and citrus segments and combine well. Spoon the mixture into a 500 ml (17 fl oz/2 cup) capacity sterilised jar with a lid and top up with enough extra oil to cover the olives. Seal and refrigerate for at least 2 days and up to 4 weeks. Bring to room temperature before eating.

1 lemon
1 blood orange
1 orange
60 ml (2 fl oz/¼ cup) olive oil, plus extra for topping
30 g (1 oz) green peppercorns in brine, drained
4 garlic cloves, thinly sliced
6 sage leaves
1 bay leaf
400 g (14 oz) Sicilian green olives

zeppole
fried anchovy dumplings

makes about 14

150 g (5½ oz/1 cup) self-raising
    (self-rising) flour,
    approximately
1 teaspoon baking powder
1 teaspoon caster (superfine)
    sugar
1 tablespoon olive oil,
    plus extra for deep-frying
200 ml (7 fl oz) milk,
    approximately
5 anchovy fillets, roughly chopped

Place the flour, baking powder, sugar and a pinch each of sea salt and freshly ground black pepper in a large bowl and combine well. Make a well in the centre, add the oil, then enough milk to make a batter the consistency of very thick cream. (You may need to add a little extra flour or milk to achieve the right consistency.) Stir through the anchovies. Set the batter aside at room temperature for 30 minutes or until slightly risen.

Heat the extra oil in a large deep saucepan or deep-fryer to 160°C (315°F) or until a cube of bread dropped into the oil browns in 30 seconds. Using a small ice-cream scoop, scoop up tablespoons of batter and carefully drop into the hot oil. Cook, turning regularly, until golden all over. Drain on absorbent paper, sprinkle with salt and serve warm.

salmone ubriaco
sugar-cured salmon with pickled beetroot

serves 4–6

Process the beetroot in a food processor until finely chopped. Add the sugar and cider and process until well combined and smooth. Transfer to a bowl.

Place the salt, herb stalks, coriander roots, garlic and chilli in a large mortar and pound with a pestle into a coarse paste. Add to the beetroot mixture and combine well.

Place the salmon in a shallow ceramic dish. Pour over the beetroot mixture, making sure the fish is completely covered. Cover with plastic wrap and refrigerate overnight.

Remove the salmon from the dish, wipe off the mixture and pat dry with absorbent paper. Using a large sharp knife, thinly slice the salmon and place in a single layer on a plate. Serve with lemon slices.

125 g (4½ oz) drained tinned whole baby beetroot

200 g (7 oz) caster (superfine) sugar

150 ml (5 fl oz) dry apple cider

200 g (7 oz) sea salt flakes

8 flat-leaf (Italian) parsley stalks, chopped

8 basil stalks, chopped

8 coriander roots, washed well and chopped

1 small garlic clove

½ long red chilli, seeds removed and finely chopped

400 g (14 oz) piece of salmon fillet, skin removed, pin-boned and blood line trimmed

lemon slices, to serve

zeppole al cavolfiore
fried cauliflower dumplings

serves 8–10

1 head cauliflower
(about 700 g/1 lb 9 oz)
500 ml (17 fl oz/2 cups) pouring
(single) cream
25 g (1 oz) dried active yeast
3 teaspoons caster (superfine)
sugar
3 teaspoons sea salt flakes
1 tablespoon olive oil
150 g (5½ oz/1 cup) plain
(all-purpose) flour
vegetable oil, for deep-frying

Cut the cauliflower into 2 cm (¾ inch) pieces and place in a small deep saucepan. Pour over the cream, cover and cook over low heat for 15 minutes or until the cauliflower begins to fall apart. Pour into a sieve placed over a bowl. Set the cream aside until cooled to room temperature.

Meanwhile, process the cauliflower in a blender until smooth. Set aside.

Place the cooled cream, yeast, sugar, salt and olive oil in a bowl and stand until frothy. Add the flour and cauliflower purée and combine well. The mixture should be sticky, elastic and run off the back of a spoon. Cover with a tea towel and stand for 30 minutes or until doubled in size.

Heat the vegetable oil in a large deep saucepan or deep-fryer to 160°C (315°F) or until a cube of bread dropped into the oil browns in 30 seconds. Using 2 tablespoons, gently drop tablespoons of batter, in batches, into the hot oil and cook for 2 minutes or until golden all over. Do not overcrowd the pan. Remove using tongs and drain on absorbent paper. Serve hot.

Baccalà is salt-cured cod usually imported from Norway. To use the salt cod it must first be soaked in several changes of fresh cold water for 2 days to rinse away the salt. You can find it at European delis.

frittelle di baccalà
salt cod fritters

makes 16–18

Place the potato in a saucepan of cold, lightly salted water and bring to the boil. Cook until tender. Drain, then mash until smooth and set aside.

Meanwhile, place the milk and garlic in a saucepan and bring to a simmer. Drain the cod and add to the pan, along with the blue-eye and simmer gently for 10 minutes or until the blue-eye is just cooked. Drain and discard the milk. Flake the fish into a large bowl and remove any skin and bones. Finely chop the garlic, add to the fish and allow to cool.

Add the mashed potato, egg yolks and mustard to the cooled fish mixture and combine well. Add the chives, season to taste with sea salt and freshly ground black pepper and combine again. Using slightly damp hands, shape tablespoons of mixture into rounds and place on a baking tray lined with baking paper.

Place the flour, beaten egg and breadcrumbs in separate shallow bowls. Dust the cod fritters in the flour, dip in the egg, allowing the excess to drain, then coat in the breadcrumbs.

Heat 1 cm (½ inch) of the oil in a large deep frying pan over medium heat. Cook the cod fritters, in batches, until golden all over. Remove with tongs and drain on absorbent paper. Serve hot.

140 g (5 oz) peeled desiree potato, chopped
300 ml (10½ fl oz) milk
3 garlic cloves
200 g (7 oz) piece of salt cod fillet, soaked in cold water for 48 hours with the water changed 4 times
200 g (7 oz) piece of blue-eye trevalla fillet
3 egg yolks
1 tablespoon Dijon mustard
20 g (¾ oz/⅓ cup) finely snipped chives
75 g (2¾ oz/½ cup) plain (all-purpose) flour, for dusting
4 eggs, lightly beaten
160 g (5¾ oz/2 cups) fresh breadcrumbs
olive oil, for shallow-frying

This olive dish comes from Filippo Navarra from the Conca D'oro Events Centre in Sydney. He is an icon in the Italian community and one of my first jobs was working for him.

olive fritte
fried sweet black olives

serves 4

Place the olives and oil in a large frying pan over low heat and cook until warm. Add the herbs and cook for another 3–4 minutes or until the olives puff up. Add the sambuca and sugar and carefully ignite the alcohol by tilting the pan towards the flame, if cooking with a gas flame, or use a lighter. When the flames die down, transfer the olives to a bowl and serve warm.

250 g (9 oz) semi-dried black olives
50 ml (1½ fl oz) olive oil
1 bay leaf
1 rosemary sprig
1 thyme sprig
80 ml (2½ fl oz/⅓ cup) white sambuca
50 g (1¾ oz) caster (superfine) sugar

ricotta infornata
baked ricotta

makes 12

Preheat the oven to 140°C (275°F/Gas 1). Line a 12-hole standard muffin tin with baking paper.
   Pat the ricotta dry with absorbent paper to remove any excess moisture. Fill the lined muffin tin with ricotta and sprinkle the salt over each. Bake for 2 hours or until semi-hard and golden. Remove from the muffin tray and allow to cool. Serve at room temperature.

750 g (1 lb 10 oz) fresh ricotta
45 g (1½ oz) sea salt flakes

giardiniera
pickled vegetables

fills one 750 ml (26 fl oz/3 cup) capacity jar

2 small carrots
2 stalks celery
½ bunch snake (yard-long) beans
    or 100 g (3½ oz) green beans
125 g (4½ oz/1 cup) cauliflower
    florets
1 small red onion
600 ml (21 fl oz) white wine vinegar
3 garlic cloves
2 thyme sprigs
4–5 parsley sprigs
4–5 basil sprigs
300 ml (10½ fl oz) olive oil,
    approximately
flat-leaf (Italian) parsley leaves,
    for garnish

Cut the carrots, celery and beans into finger-length pieces. Cut the cauliflower into small florets and thickly slice the onion.

Place the vinegar in a large saucepan and slowly bring to the boil over medium heat. Add the vegetables, garlic and herb sprigs. Bring back to the boil, then remove from the heat and allow the vegetables to cool in the vinegar.

Strain the cooled vegetables in a sieve placed over a bowl and reserve 150 ml (5 fl oz) of the vinegar. Place the vegetables, garlic and herb sprigs in a 750 ml (26 fl oz/3 cup) capacity sterilised jar with a lid.

Combine the oil and the reserved vinegar. Pour over the vegetables and top up with a little extra oil, if necessary, so there is no air left at the top of the jar. Seal the jar.

Place a heavy upturned plate in the base of a large saucepan. Place the jar on top and cover well with cold water. Cook over very low heat until the water temperature reaches 70°C (150°F). The water should be just simmering, not at all boiling. Keep the temperature at 70°C for 3 hours, then remove the pan from the heat and allow the jar to cool in the water. Drain, dry the jar with a tea towel and refrigerate for at least 1 week and up to 6 months. Once opened, make sure the giardiniera is always covered in oil and it will keep for up to 2 weeks in the refrigerator.

To serve, take out the desired amount, season to taste with sea salt and freshly ground black pepper and scatter over some parsley.

a lasting harvest

Growing up there was always something delicious in a jar in a small cupboard under the sink. The cupboard was full of big, colourful jars of pickled and preserved fruit and vegetables. I cherished them then and still do now. Mum constantly had a whole array of pickled and preserved food available; it meant having the best produce in peak condition all year round.

I still follow the recipes taught to me by my mum. I pickle vegetables with a hot vinegar, oil and herb dressing to keep their crunch and natural colour. I love anything pickled, from cauliflower and eggplant (aubergine) to snake (yard-long) beans, tomatoes and chillies.

Preserving is slightly different from pickling. It's a slow-cooking process used to preserve either whole fruit or vegetables, crushed tomatoes or eggplants, or to make sauces, chutney or jam. Mum also dried fruit in the sun — a snack I loved as a kid.

Mum usually made the preserves on her own, except for one: passata (crushed tomatoes). Passata making is a big, annual event for most southern Italians and their entire families (even in Australia). It's a way of preserving tomatoes in peak season to retain their most intense flavours. It's a long but always fun day, and by sunset there are usually more than 2,000 old-fashioned beer bottles full of the most incredible red tomato sauce.

Pickled and preserved foods can be pulled straight out of the jar, put on a plate and eaten with crusty bread. It's the perfect snack which brings back a lot of memories for me. For dinner, pickles are generally eaten at the beginning of the meal to get the appetite going because vinegar makes you thirsty and hungry. Preserves are usually served within the meal as we graze or served after the main meal with cheese.

arancini
deep-fried rice balls

makes about 30

Preheat the oven to 160°C (315°F/Gas 2–3).

Place the stock in a saucepan, bring to the boil, then reduce the heat to low and keep at a bare simmer.

Heat the olive oil in a heavy-based ovenproof saucepan over low–medium heat. Add the onion and cook for 3–4 minutes or until translucent. Add the garlic and cook for another 1–2 minutes. Add the rice and stir for 1–2 minutes or until the grains are well coated. Add the stock, 125 ml (4 fl oz/½ cup) at a time, allowing each addition to be absorbed before adding the next and stir continuously. Once all but 125 ml of the stock has been added, remove from the heat and stir in the remaining stock. Cover with a lid or foil and bake for 20 minutes or until the rice is cooked through but not al dente.

Remove from the oven, stir in the Napoletana sauce, cheeses and basil and combine well. Season to taste with sea salt and freshly ground black pepper. Spread the rice over a large tray, cover with plastic wrap and refrigerate until completely cold.

Using slightly damp hands, roll the mixture into golf-ball-sized balls and place on a baking tray lined with baking paper. Place the flour, beaten egg and breadcrumbs in separate shallow bowls. Dust the arancini in flour, dip in the egg, allowing the excess to drain, then coat in the breadcrumbs. Place back on the tray and refrigerate for 15 minutes or until firm.

Heat the canola oil in a large deep saucepan or deep-fryer to 160°C (315°F) or until a cube of bread dropped into the oil browns in 30 seconds. Deep-fry the arancini, in batches, until golden all over. Remove using a slotted spoon and drain on absorbent paper. Serve warm or cold.

650 ml (22½ fl oz) vegetable stock (see page 265)
60 ml (2 fl oz/¼ cup) olive oil
½ small brown onion, finely chopped
1 garlic clove, thinly sliced
150 g (5½ oz) arborio rice (see page 140)
150 ml (5 fl oz) Napoletana sauce (see page 262)
100 g (3½ oz/1 cup) finely grated parmesan
50 g (1¾ oz) buffalo mozzarella, chopped
5 basil leaves, finely chopped
50 g (1¾ oz/⅓ cup) plain (all-purpose) flour
3 eggs, lightly beaten
150 g (5½ oz/1½ cups) dry fine breadcrumbs
canola oil, for deep-frying

olive schiacciate
crushed olives

serves 4–6

300 g (10½ oz) Sicilian green
   olives
150 ml (5 fl oz) olive oil
1 onion, finely chopped
1 stalk celery, finely chopped
1 garlic clove, thinly sliced
80 ml (2½ fl oz/⅓ cup) lemon
   juice
1 small handful flat-leaf (Italian)
   parsley leaves, chopped

Using the flat side of a large knife, crush the olives on a chopping board and remove the pits. Place the olives in a bowl and set aside.

Heat 2 tablespoons of the oil in a heavy-based saucepan over medium heat. Add the onion, celery and garlic and cook for 6–8 minutes or until starting to caramelise. Remove from the heat and allow to cool.

Add the cooled onion mixture to the olives, along with the lemon juice, parsley and remaining oil. Season to taste with sea salt and freshly ground black pepper and serve at room temperature.

The schiacciate will keep for 7 days stored in an airtight container in the refrigerator.

budino al tartufo estivo
summer truffle tartlets

makes 8

To make the sour cream shortcrust pastry, place the flour, butter, sour cream, egg white and a pinch of sea salt in a food processor and process until it just comes together. Turn out onto a lightly floured surface and shape into a disc. Wrap in plastic wrap and refrigerate for 30 minutes.

Preheat the oven to 180°C (350°F/Gas 4).

Roll out the dough to 4–5 mm (⅛–¼ inch) thick between sheets of baking paper. Use a 9 cm (3½ inch) round pastry cutter to cut out rounds and use these to line 6 cm (2½ inch) loose-bottomed tartlet tins. Line the pastry cases with baking paper, fill with baking weights, such as uncooked rice or dried beans, and blind bake for 15 minutes. Remove the paper and weights, return to the oven and bake for another 5 minutes or until lightly golden. Set cases aside. Reduce the temperature to 150°C (300°F/Gas 2).

To make the filling, place the egg yolks, cream and truffle in a bowl, season with sea salt and freshly ground black pepper to taste and whisk until combined. Remove any froth from the top, then pour the filling into the pastry cases.

Bake for about 12 minutes or until the filling is firm. Remove from the oven and allow the tartlets to rest in their tins, cool, then gently remove them from their tins. Sprinkle the tops with sugar and use a kitchen blowtorch to caramelise the sugar. Serve immediately at room temperature.

Note Summer truffle is a great addition to this dish. In Italy, nearly every family uses summer truffles in their cooking. They are not considered a luxury like winter truffles because their flavour is less intense.

5 eggs yolks
300 ml (10½ fl oz) pouring (single) cream
50 g (1¾ oz) summer truffle (see Note), shaved
caster (superfine) sugar, for brûléeing

sour cream shortcrust pastry
200 g (7 oz/1⅓ cups) plain (all-purpose) flour, plus extra for dusting
120 g (4¼ oz) unsalted butter, chilled and diced
50 g (1¾ oz) sour cream
1 egg white

acciughe ripiene
stuffed sardines

serves 6–8

Preheat the oven to 160°C (315°F/Gas 2–3).

Place the breadcrumbs, egg yolk, parsley, provolone and semi-dried tomatoes in a bowl, season to taste with sea salt and freshly ground black pepper and stir to combine until a thick paste forms.

Place the sardines, skin-side down, on a work surface and place 1 heaped teaspoon of the breadcrumb mixture along one half of each sardine. Fold the sardines over and secure with kitchen string.

Heat the oil in a large heavy-based frying pan over medium heat. Cook the sardines, in batches, for 1 minute each side or until golden. Remove from the pan, place in a baking dish and bake for 6 minutes or until just cooked through. Remove from the oven and set aside.

In the same frying pan, add the onion and cook over high heat for 3–4 minutes or until translucent. Add the vinegar and sugar and cook, stirring, for 6–8 minutes or until dry. Spoon over the sardines and serve at room temperature.

20 g (¾ oz/¼ cup) fresh breadcrumbs

1 egg yolk

2 tablespoons coarsely chopped flat-leaf (Italian) parsley leaves

25 g (1 oz) provolone, coarsely grated

1 tablespoon finely chopped semi-dried tomatoes

14 butterflied sardines

2 tablespoons olive oil

1 small brown onion, finely chopped

100 ml (3½ fl oz) balsamic vinegar

100 g (3½ oz) caster (superfine) sugar

polpette
meatballs

serves 6

200 g (7 oz) minced (ground) pork
(ask your butcher for a
60% meat to 40% fat ratio
on a 1 cm/½ inch grind)
80 g (2¾ oz) minced (ground) veal
(ask your butcher for
a 1 cm/½ inch grind)
1 small handful flat-leaf (Italian)
parsley leaves, chopped
50 g (1¾ oz/½ cup) finely grated
parmesan
20 g (¾ oz/¼ cup) fresh
breadcrumbs
3 egg yolks
60 ml (2 fl oz/¼ cup) red wine
olive oil, for shallow-frying

Place all the ingredients except the oil in a bowl,
season to taste with sea salt and freshly ground
black pepper and, using your hands, combine well.

Shape heaped teaspoons of the mixture into
balls, place on a work surface and press down
gently to make flat ovals so they cook evenly.

Heat 1 cm (½ inch) of oil in a large frying pan
over medium heat. Cook the meatballs, in batches,
until golden all over. Remove with a slotted spoon
and drain on absorbent paper. Serve warm or at
room temperature.

These olives make a great versatile assaggino as you can use any of your favourite fillings. I usually let my fridge decide for me. I'll raid the fridge and use any leftovers as a filling — Bolognese sauce, last night's lamb shanks or anything else that is cold and firm is best.

olive farcite di ricotta
crumbed ricotta-filled olives

serves 6–8

Place the ricotta, parmesan, egg yolk and truffle paste in a bowl. Season to taste with sea salt and freshly ground black pepper and combine well.

Transfer the ricotta mixture to a piping bag fitted with a 1 cm (½ inch) plain nozzle and fill the olive cavities with the mixture. Do not overfill or they will pop when you cook them.

Place the flour, beaten egg and breadcrumbs in separate shallow bowls. Dust the olives in flour, dip in the egg, allowing the excess to drain, then coat in the crumbs. Place on a baking tray lined with baking paper and refrigerate for 1 hour.

Heat the oil in a large deep saucepan or deep-fryer to 150°C (300°F) or until a cube of bread dropped into the oil browns in 25 seconds. Deep-fry the olives, in batches, until golden and crisp. Remove with a slotted spoon, drain on absorbent paper and serve warm.

100 g (3½ oz) ricotta
30 g (1 oz) finely grated parmesan
1 egg yolk
1 teaspoon truffle paste
400 g (14 oz) pitted jumbo green olives
75 g (2¾ oz/½ cup) plain (all-purpose) flour
3 eggs, lightly beaten
200 g (7 oz/2 cups) dry fine breadcrumbs
500 ml (17 fl oz/2 cups) canola oil, for deep-frying

sbrise
crumbed oyster mushrooms

serves 4

200 g (7 oz) oyster mushrooms
canola oil, for deep-frying
175 g (6 oz/1 cup) tapioca flour
good-quality mayonnaise,
    for dipping

Using a slightly damp cloth, wipe any dirt or grit off the mushrooms and trim any woody stems. Bring a large saucepan of lightly salted water to the boil and blanch the mushrooms for 1½ minutes or until tender. Drain and refresh in iced water. Drain again and pat dry with a tea towel. Thickly slice lengthways.

Heat the oil in a large deep saucepan or deep-fryer until 180°C (350°F) or until a cube of bread dropped into the oil browns in 15 seconds. Lightly dust the mushrooms with the flour, shaking off the excess. Deep-fry for 3 minutes or until lightly golden and crisp. Remove with a slotted spoon and drain on absorbent paper. Sprinkle with sea salt and serve hot with mayonnaise for dipping.

This is a good basic recipe for Italian sausages. I always ask my butcher to coarsely grind my meat instead of buying the pre-minced stuff, so I know exactly what's in it. Don't be scared of the amount of fat in this mixture as this is what will keep the sausages juicy. The quantities need to be exact otherwise the meat will be too salty or bland. The trick to making sausages that don't burst when you cook them is to prick them all over with a pin just after you've made them. Another trick is to begin cooking them in cold oil in a cold pan — never add sausages to a really hot pan or they will pop.

salsicce
italian sausages

makes about 12

Place the pork, spices and wine in a large bowl and, using your hands, combine very well. Cover and refrigerate for at least 12 hours.

Check the mixture is not too dry. Add a little more wine, if necessary. Half fill a piping bag fitted with a 3 cm (1¼ inch) plain nozzle with the mixture.

Tie a knot at one end of the casing. Place the other end of the casing over the piping bag nozzle and thread the entire length of casing onto the nozzle until you reach the knot. Pipe the mixture in a coiling motion into the casing, using one hand to make sure the end doesn't slip off the piping bag nozzle. Refill the piping bag with mixture as you go.

Press along the length of the casing to remove any air pockets and to make sure the mixture is even. Make sure the casing isn't filled too tight or the sausages will pop when cooked. Twist the filled casing in one direction at 12 cm (4½ inch) intervals to form sausages. Prick the sausages with a fine pin or needle all over. Place on a tray and refrigerate, uncovered, for 1 hour.

Place the oil and sausages in a large cold frying pan. Place over medium heat and cook, turning regularly, for 5–6 minutes or until cooked through and golden. Enjoy hot in an Italian bread roll.

1 kg (2 lb 4 oz) minced (ground) pork (ask your butcher for a 60% meat to 40% fat ratio on a 1 cm/½ inch grind)
6 g (⅕ oz) fennel seeds
20 g (¾ oz) sea salt flakes
8 g (⅓ oz) freshly ground black pepper
80 ml (2½ fl oz/⅓ cup) light-bodied red wine, approximately
1 metre (39½ inches) cleaned sausage casing (pig's intestine) (ask your butcher for this)
2 tablespoons olive oil
Italian bread rolls, to serve

frittelle di nannata
whitebait fritters

makes about 18

270 g (9½ oz) fresh or frozen
   whitebait
2 eggs
1½ tablespoons coarsely chopped
   flat-leaf (Italian) parsley leaves
1½ tablespoons finely grated
   parmesan
zest of ½ lemon
50 g (1¾ oz/⅓ cup) plain
   (all-purpose) flour
olive oil, for shallow-frying
lemon wedges, to serve

Rinse the whitebait under cold running water to ensure there is no seaweed or any other impurities. Transfer to a colander placed over a bowl and refrigerate for up to 2 hours to drain the excess water.

Place the eggs, parsley, parmesan and lemon zest in a bowl and combine well. Add the whitebait and flour. Season to taste with sea salt and freshly ground black pepper and combine well.

Heat 1 cm (½ inch) of oil in a large deep frying pan over medium–high heat. Cook tablespoons of the mixture, in small batches, for 2–3 minutes each side or until golden all over and the centre is soft but not runny. Remove with a slotted spoon and drain on absorbent paper. Sprinkle with salt and serve hot with lemon wedges or cold tossed through a crisp salad.

This recipe uses frozen porcini mushrooms, which you can buy from gourmet food stores or any good Italian deli. If you're lucky enough to get hold of fresh porcini, then use them instead. The panna cottas taste just as good with any of your favourite mushrooms, particularly button.

panna cotta ai funghi porcini
porcini mushroom panna cotta

makes 4

Heat the olive oil in a heavy-based saucepan over low–medium heat. Add the onion and garlic and cook for 4–5 minutes or until translucent. Add the mushrooms, season to taste with sea salt and freshly ground black pepper and cook for another 5 minutes or until all the liquid has evaporated. Add the cream, simmer for 10 minutes, then remove from the heat and stand for 10 minutes.

Process the mixture in a food processor until smooth. Push the mixture through a fine sieve, then transfer to a small clean saucepan over low heat. Cook, stirring regularly, until just warm.

Meanwhile, soak the gelatine in cold water until softened. Remove the softened gelatine from the water, squeeze out the excess water, add to the mushroom mixture and stir until dissolved. Strain through a fine sieve, then pour into four 60 ml (2 fl oz/¼ cup) capacity moulds. Cover with plastic wrap and refrigerate overnight.

Half an hour before serving, remove the panna cottas from the refrigerator. Unmould them by dipping the bases briefly in hot water and carefully invert onto serving plates. Bring to room temperature to serve. Combine the parsley and extra virgin olive oil and season. Spoon over the panna cottas just before serving.

2 tablespoons olive oil
1 small onion, finely chopped
1 garlic clove, sliced
100 g (3½ oz) frozen porcini (cep) mushrooms, defrosted and thinly sliced
300 ml (10½ fl oz) pouring (single) cream
1 leaf gold-strength gelatine
1 tablespoon finely chopped flat-leaf (Italian) parsley leaves
2 tablespoons extra virgin olive oil

frittelle di asparagi
asparagus fritters

serves 4

1 bunch baby asparagus, trimmed
3 eggs
1 tablespoon pouring (single)
     cream, approximately
70 g (2½ oz) self-raising
     (self-rising) flour, approximately
500 ml (17 fl oz/2 cups)
     vegetable oil
lemon wedges, to serve

Cut the asparagus into 1 cm (½ inch) lengths, place in a bowl and season to taste with sea salt and freshly ground black pepper.

Place the eggs and cream in a bowl and beat until just combined. While stirring continuously, slowly add the flour and combine well. The batter should just stick to the spoon. You may need to add a little extra cream or flour to achieve the right consistency. Stir in the asparagus.

Heat the oil in a large deep saucepan or deep-fryer to 160°C (315°F) or until a cube of bread dropped into the oil browns in 30 seconds. Carefully drop tablespoons of mixture into the oil, in batches, and cook until golden all over. Remove with tongs and drain on absorbent paper, sprinkle with salt and serve warm or at room temperature with lemon wedges.

antipasti
small plates for sharing

Placing these antipasti down in front of a guest would be a great way to start a lunch or dinner.
I have modernised these dishes to suit the way we live and eat today. The type of antipasti served are a good indication of the style of the chef cooking for you and is a taste of what is to come. Most contain six or more ingredients and showcase how flavoursome simple ingredients can be.

Italian meals typically start with antipasti and they are left on the table from the beginning to the end of the meal. We love to graze! Every time we sit down together as a family, we feast, not on three courses that are cleared in between, but on continual small plates. It's the way of the Mediterranean diet, everything in moderation so our bodies are constantly nourished. Any of these dishes would also make a great starter on their own, although it's easy to make up an entire meal with a few of these dishes simply served with bread.

To begin a meal, antipasti are always enjoyed with a great Lambrusco, a slightly sparkling red wine. Lambrusco is not so trendy nowadays but these wines from Emilia-Romagna and Lombardy are the best match for this type of eating. In between courses, you should have a rest, as is customary in Italian culture as there is always a lot more food to come — so don't make any appointments for afterwards! And to finish the meal, a good digestive, which we call 'amaro'.

gamberi all'aglio
garlic prawns

serves 4

Heat the oil in a large deep frying pan over high heat. Add the garlic and cook for 2 mintues or until just golden, then add the chilli and tomato. Bring to a simmer, add the basil and season to taste with sea salt and freshly ground black pepper.

Add the prawns, stir to combine and cook for 2–3 minutes or until just cooked through. Divide the prawns and sauce among small bowls and serve with crusty bread for mopping.

100 ml (3½ fl oz) olive oil
5 garlic cloves, sliced
½ long red chilli, seeds removed and thinly sliced
1 small ox heart tomato, peeled and diced
8 basil leaves, torn
12 large raw prawns (shrimp) peeled and deveined with tails left intact
crusty bread, to serve

torta di melanzana
eggplant cake

serves 8

4 medium eggplants (aubergines)
360 ml (12½ fl oz) olive oil
500 ml (17 fl oz/2 cups)
    Napoletana sauce
    (see page 262), cooled
16 basil leaves
50 g (1¾ oz) fresh breadcrumbs
150 g (5½ oz/1½ cups) finely
    grated parmesan
150 g (5½ oz) buffalo mozzarella,
    thinly sliced
4 eggs, hard-boiled, peeled
    and thinly sliced
crusty bread, to serve

Cut the eggplants lengthways into 7 mm (⅜ inch) thick slices. Heat 300 ml (10½ fl oz) of the oil in a large heavy-based frying pan over medium heat. Cook the eggplant, in batches, on both sides until golden. Drain on absorbent paper.

Place the Napoletana sauce, basil, breadcrumbs and the remaining oil in a bowl and combine well.

Preheat the oven to 140°C (275°F/Gas 1).

Line the base of a lightly greased 20 cm (8 inch) round springform cake tin with a layer of eggplant. Spread a thin layer of the sauce over the base, scatter with a little of both the cheeses and top with a layer of sliced egg. Repeat layering the remaining ingredients 2 more times, then finish with a layer of eggplant. Cover tightly with foil, making sure the foil touches the surface of the eggplant. Place on an oven tray and bake for 45 minutes, then remove the foil and bake for another 45 minutes or until the oil starts to rise to the top of the tin. Remove from the oven and allow to cool.

Cover again with foil and weight down with food tins, then refrigerate overnight to set.

To serve, remove the food tins and foil. Place a large plate on top of the cake tin, invert the tin and undo the clip. Slice the cake into wedges and serve with crusty bread.

carpaccio di polpo
octopus carpaccio serves 8

50 ml (1¾ fl oz) olive oil

500 g (1 lb 2 oz) cleaned
　　large octopus tentacles
　　(about 100 g/3½ oz each)

1 small handful flat-leaf (Italian)
　　parsley leaves, chopped

zest of ½ lemon

1 teaspoon freshly ground
　　white pepper

80 ml (2½ fl oz/⅓ cup) fish stock
　　(see page 265)

25 g (1 oz) powdered gelatine

extra virgin olive oil, for drizzling

lemon wedges, to serve

Heat the oil in a large frying pan over high heat. When very hot, add the octopus and cook for 2–3 minutes or until lightly coloured. Add the parsley, lemon zest, pepper and stock and simmer until the liquid has reduced to a sticky sauce to coat the octopus. Remove from the heat, season to taste with sea salt and cool slightly.

Lightly dampen a work surface and place a 30 cm (12 inch) long piece of plastic wrap on top. Repeat dampening and layering to make 5–6 layers — the dampening stops the plastic from slipping. While the octopus is still hot, lay the tentacles alternately, top to tail, in a 15 cm (6 inch) log shape and sprinkle over the gelatine. Roll up to secure, press down firmly to remove any air bubbles, then secure the ends tightly and refrigerate overnight.

Using a very shape knife, cut the roll into 8 mm (⅜ inch) thick slices, then unwrap and arrange on a plate. Drizzle with the extra virgin olive oil, season to taste and serve with the lemon wedges.

carpaccio di salmone
salmon carpaccio serves 4

250 g (9 oz) piece of salmon fillet,
　　skin removed, pin-boned and
　　blood line trimmed

100 g (3½ oz) olive schiacciate
　　(see page 30), finely chopped

50 g (1¾ oz) ricotta infornata
　　(see page 23)

extra virgin olive oil, for drizzling

crusty bread, to serve

Slice the salmon very thinly against the grain and arrange on 4 serving plates.

Top with the olive schiacciate, then crumble over the ricotta infornata. Season to taste with sea salt and freshly ground black pepper, drizzle with the oil and serve with crusty bread.

carpaccio di manzo
beef carpaccio serves 4

Cover a dinner plate with a piece of plastic wrap. Using a large sharp knife, thinly slice the beef fillet against the grain. Arrange one-quarter of the beef on the prepared plate in a spiral pattern beginning in the centre until half of the plate is covered. Take another piece of plastic wrap and cover the beef. Slide the plastic and beef onto a chopping board, then lightly bash the meat with the flat side of a meat mallet or roll with a rolling pin until it flattens out enough to cover the entire plate. Peel off the top layer of plastic wrap and flip the beef onto the plate. Keep the other piece of plastic wrap on the beef and refrigerate until just before serving. Repeat with the remaining beef.

Heat the olive oil in a non-stick frying pan over medium–high heat. Crumble the sausage meat into the pan and stir, breaking the meat up with the back of a spoon, for about 4–5 minutes or until well browned and crisp. Add the semi-dried tomatoes, stir to combine, then remove from the heat and cool.

Toss the rocket with the extra virgin olive oil and lemon juice and season to taste with sea salt and freshly ground black pepper.

To serve, peel the plastic wrap off the beef, spoon the cooled pork mixture over the top, then scatter with the rocket and parmesan.

200 g (7 oz) piece of best
    end-beef fillet
1½ tablespoons olive oil
75 g (2¾ oz) Italian pork and
    fennel sausage, casing
    removed
6 semi-dried tomatoes
35 g (1¼ oz/1 cup) wild rocket
    (arugula) leaves
1½ tablespoons extra virgin
    olive oil
juice of 1 small lemon
25 g (1 oz/¼ cup) shaved
    parmesan

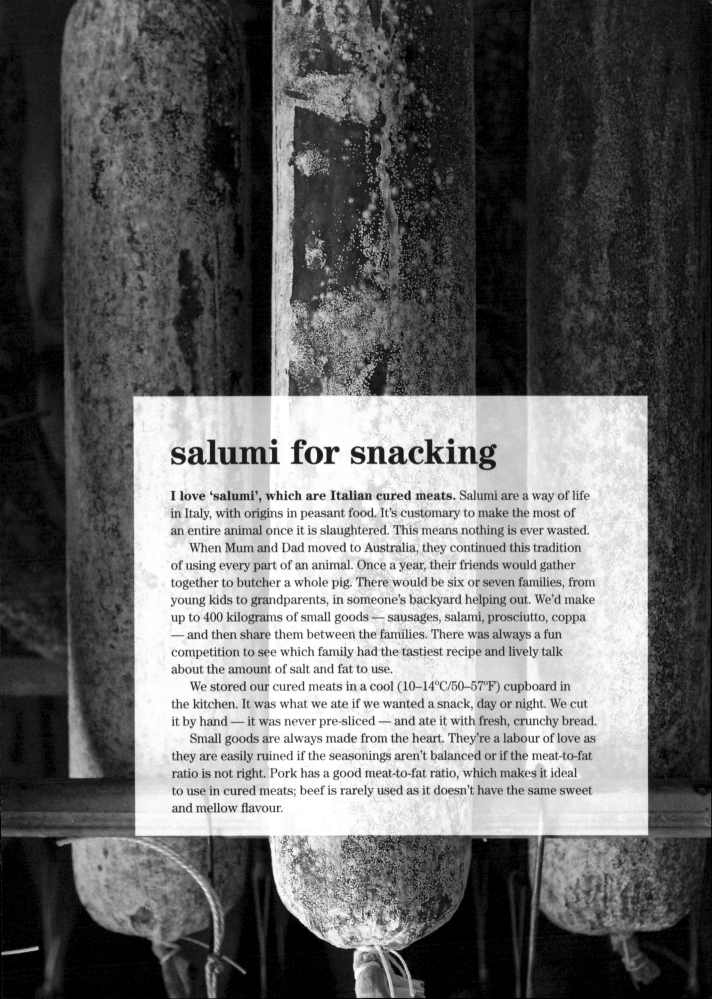

salumi for snacking

I love 'salumi', which are Italian cured meats. Salumi are a way of life in Italy, with origins in peasant food. It's customary to make the most of an entire animal once it is slaughtered. This means nothing is ever wasted.

When Mum and Dad moved to Australia, they continued this tradition of using every part of an animal. Once a year, their friends would gather together to butcher a whole pig. There would be six or seven families, from young kids to grandparents, in someone's backyard helping out. We'd make up to 400 kilograms of small goods — sausages, salami, prosciutto, coppa — and then share them between the families. There was always a fun competition to see which family had the tastiest recipe and lively talk about the amount of salt and fat to use.

We stored our cured meats in a cool (10–14°C/50–57°F) cupboard in the kitchen. It was what we ate if we wanted a snack, day or night. We cut it by hand — it was never pre-sliced — and ate it with fresh, crunchy bread.

Small goods are always made from the heart. They're a labour of love as they are easily ruined if the seasonings aren't balanced or if the meat-to-fat ratio is not right. Pork has a good meat-to-fat ratio, which makes it ideal to use in cured meats; beef is rarely used as it doesn't have the same sweet and mellow flavour.

fat is flavour As a kid, salami would be made up of 40 per cent fat, as I grew up it became 20 per cent and now it's 10 per cent. Despite today's health-conscious society, I make my small goods with up to 40 per cent fat because sausages without fat have no flavour. At my restaurant, I serve my own cured meats, including salami, cacciatore, coppa and pancetta.

italian deli shopping For the best-quality cured meats, look for smaller, boutique brands, as big brands tend to use preservatives. Make sure the product looks clean and fresh; if you're not sure, ask how long it's been in the counter or look at the date when it was made on the label. Don't accept meat from the end; instead ask your grocer for a new one, to cut it in half and begin slicing it from the middle. Variety is key — a few slices of 10 different meats gets the taste buds going.

pancetta Italians use pancetta in many different recipes, from soups and braises to pasta and rice. It's made from pork belly and is the easiest to make as it's simply peppered, salted and cured for three months. To really appreciate its flavour, though, the best way to eat it is thinly sliced at room temperature.

coppa To make coppa, pork neck or shoulder is usually marinated in red wine and herbs, then salted, hung to dry and cured for six months in a net. I enjoy it sliced very thinly in a sandwich with pickled vegetables.

prosciutto Made from pork leg, prosciutto is one of the hardest salumi to make because it's cured on the bone, which increases its potential to go rancid. Once the bone is removed, the leg is pressed again and reset, then cured in a cool cellar for 9–18 months. You must slice it thinly to appreciate its delicate flavour.

salami Usually made from pork shoulder and other off-cuts, you'll find that different regions add their own local ingredients, such as fennel or chilli (from Calabria), garlic (from Sicily) or white truffles (from Piedmont or Milan). I prefer to add salt, pepper and white wine. The salami are then hung at room temperature for up to a year.

cacciatore Also made from pork shoulder and other off-cuts, this is a semi-cured salami (meaning it's only hung for one month). It is then placed in a jar of olive oil and left to marinate for six months. The real beauty of this style of cured meat is that you can use the infused oil for cooking.

mortadella Today this is mainly made from pork which is processed into a mousse, but traditionally it was made from horse and donkey meat. Herbs, spices and aromatics are added, it is then cooked and slowly smoked for 15–48 hours, depending on the size.

cotechino This is a fresh, not cured, meat and is traditionally eaten on New Year's Day. Every part of meat on the pig's head is taken off the bone, minced, then put into a casing. It is then poached for 3–4 hours.

focaccia con olive e acciughe
olive & sardine focaccia

serves 6

5 butterflied sardines
sea salt flakes
200 ml (7 fl oz) milk
40 g (1½ oz) fresh yeast
    (see Note), crumbled
185 ml (6 fl oz/¾ cup) olive oil
2 teaspoons caster (superfine)
    sugar
400 g (14 oz) strong bread (00)
    flour, plus extra for dusting
60 g (2¼ oz/½ cup) small pitted
    black olives

Halve each sardine lengthways so you have 10 fillets. Place in a shallow dish, sprinkle lightly with sea salt on both sides, cover with plastic wrap and refrigerate for 3 hours. Rinse off the salt, then place in a dish with the milk and refrigerate for another 1 hour.

Strain the sardines in a sieve placed over a bowl, reserving the milk. Refrigerate the sardines until needed. Heat the milk in a small saucepan over low heat until lukewarm (30°C/86°F), then transfer to a small bowl. Add the yeast, 60 ml (2 fl oz/¼ cup) of the oil and the sugar and stir to combine well. Stand in a warm place for 10 minutes or until the mixture begins to foam.

Place the flour and 3 teaspoons sea salt in a large bowl. Add the yeast mixture and stir until a dough forms. If it's a little dry, add a touch of water. Turn out onto a lightly floured surface and knead for 10 minutes or until smooth and elastic. Place in a well-oiled 24 cm (9½ inch) round cake tin, stretching the dough out with your fingers to cover the base. Cover with a tea towel and stand in a warm place until doubled in size.

Roll the sardines widthways, then push them and the olives deep into the dough. Brush the focaccia with a little of the remaining oil and stand in a warm place until risen by half.

Preheat the oven to 170°C (325°F/Gas 3). Brush the focaccia again with a little oil and bake for 2 hours, brushing regularly with the remaining oil. It's ready when it is crusty on top but moist in the centre. Remove from the oven, stand for 15 minutes in the tin, then turn out, cut and enjoy hot.

Note Fresh yeast is available from health food stores, Italian delis and bakeries.

calamari ripieni
stuffed calamari in sauce

serves 6

Cut the ciabatta into slices and toast on both sides. Cool, then place in a food processor and process until coarse breadcrumbs form. Transfer to a bowl and set aside.

Place the fish fillets in a food processor and process until smooth. Set aside.

Heat 2 tablespoons of the oil in a frying pan over low–medium heat. Add the onion and garlic and cook for 4–5 minutes or until lightly caramelised. Add half of the wine and simmer until reduced and sticky. Add three-quarters of the parsley and simmer for another 2 minutes. Transfer to a bowl and allow to cool. Add the breadcrumbs, fish purée and chopped egg to the cooled onion mixture, season to taste with sea salt and freshly ground black pepper and combine well. Do not overwork or the stuffing will be too dense. If the stuffing seems a little dry, add a little extra wine.

Preheat the oven to 160°C (315°F/Gas 2–3).

Spoon the stuffing into the calamari tubes, making sure not to overfill them or they will split during cooking. Secure the ends with toothpicks.

Place the remaining oil and the calamari in a large cold ovenproof frying pan and place over medium heat. Cook the calamari until they are just opaque all over. Add the remaining wine, then bake for 15 minutes or until just cooked through. Remove the calamari from the pan and set aside. Add the butter and remaining parsley to the pan and season to taste. Swirl the butter, then return the calamari to the pan and gently coat with the sauce.

Note River calamari live in freshwater and are smaller than their seawater cousins. There is no need to remove their skins when preparing them.

100 g (3½ oz) ciabatta bread
(see page 74)
100 g (3½ oz) skinless
white-fleshed fish fillets
100 ml (3½ fl oz) olive oil
1 onion, finely chopped
2 garlic cloves, thinly sliced
80 ml (2½ fl oz/⅓ cup) white wine
2 tablespoons coarsely chopped
flat-leaf (Italian) parsley leaves
2 eggs, hard-boiled, peeled
and chopped
6 river calamari tubes (each
about 8 cm/3¼ inches long),
cleaned (see Note)
60 g (2¼ oz) butter

terrina di guanciale fritto
crumbed ox cheek terrine

serves 8

125 ml (4 fl oz/½ cup) olive oil

300 g (10½ oz) ox cheek, cut into
2 cm (¾ inch) thick slices

1 small carrot, finely diced

1 small stalk celery, finely diced

1 small onion, finely diced

2 garlic cloves, chopped

250 ml (9 fl oz/1cup) white wine

150 ml (5 fl oz) chicken stock
(see page 264)

320 g (11¼ oz/4 cups) fresh
breadcrumbs

1 large handful flat-leaf (Italian)
parsley leaves, chopped

zest of 1 lemon

zest of ½ orange

seasoned plain (all-purpose) flour,
for dusting

4 eggs, lightly beaten

extra virgin olive oil, for drizzling

Preheat the oven to 170°C (325°F/Gas 3). Heat 60 ml (2 fl oz/¼ cup) of the olive oil in a large heavy-based ovenproof saucepan over medium–high heat. Cook the ox cheek until browned all over, then remove from the pan and set aside. Add the remaining oil to the pan, along with the vegetables and garlic and cook for 5 minutes or until just softened. Add the wine and deglaze the pan, scraping the base to remove any cooked-on pieces and simmer until reduced by two-thirds. Return the cheek to the pan, add the stock and season to taste with sea salt and freshly ground black pepper. Bring to a simmer, then cover and bake for 4 hours or until the meat is very tender. Remove the cheek slices from the pan, then place the pan over low heat and simmer until the liquid is reduced and sticky. Return the cheek slices to the pan and turn to coat well. Transfer to a container, cool, then cover and refrigerate overnight.

Preheat the oven to 130°C (250°F/Gas 1). Process the breadcrumbs, parsley and citrus zest in a food processor until just combined. Spread on a baking tray and bake for 6–8 minutes or until dry but not coloured. Cool, then process again until fine. Using a 4–5 cm (1½–2 inch) biscuit cutter, mould the cheek slices into rounds and place on a baking tray lined with baking paper. Place the seasoned flour, beaten egg and breadcrumb mixture in separate shallow bowls. Dust the cheek pieces in the flour, dip in the egg, allowing the excess to drain, then coat in the breadcrumb mixture. Place back on the tray and refrigerate for 2 hours or until firm.

Preheat the oven to 180°C (350°F/Gas 4). Bake the rounds for 12–15 minutes or until lightly golden. Drizzle with extra virgin olive oil to serve.

pasta di pane

My parents grew up in Catania in Sicily and, like many other Italian peasants, survived mainly on fresh bread. Bread was the cheapest thing you could make. They instilled in me an appreciation of bread and it's a fundamental part of my diet today. Growing up, Mum and Dad used unrefined flour which they ground themselves. Refined flours and yeast were considered a luxury, so the bread they always baked was a coarse flatbread with massive holes and lots of flavour.

'La vera cucina' (real Italian cooking) comes from the heart, not the head. It's what real food is about. Every Saturday morning was baking day. When it was time to make bread, six or seven mums would get together and crush the wheat using a stone-ground mill. The ground flour was then mixed with a little water to make a basic dough. They, and the rest of the township, would take their dough to the communal wood-fired oven in the piazza. Whenever Mum and Dad tell me these stories, I can only imagine the food and the smells around the piazza.

Sometimes olive oil would be added to the dough, or a few olives and a bit of pork thrown in, then the dough flattened out. That's how focaccia bread and pizza came about, with peasants making the most of their local food. 'Mafalda', a common Sicilian word used to describe traditional bread, pasta and other dishes, translates as 'badly made', which sounds like an unfavourable description but perfectly describes this simple, rough style of cooking.

During that time, northern Italy was wealthier than the south, so they could afford to mill their wheat and add yeast, which is why they baked larger loaves.

At my restaurant, I only serve old-fashioned, homemade bread, like my ciabatta (see page 74) or sardine and olive focaccia (see page 62). I add olive oil, just like my mum, or sometimes ricotta in the mix, to lighten the dough and make it more moist.

parfait al fegato con vincotto e pane al finocchio
liver parfait with vincotto & fennel bread
serves 6–8

liver parfait

2 tablespoons olive oil

150 g (5½ oz) white onion, finely chopped

100 g (3½ oz) cleaned chicken livers

60 ml (2 fl oz/¼ cup) brandy

130 g (4¾ oz) butter, chopped

30 ml (1 fl oz) vincotto

fennel bread

115 ml (3¾ fl oz) warm milk

12 g (⅖ oz) caster (superfine) sugar

15 g (½ oz) fresh yeast (see Note)

2 teaspoons olive oil

1 teaspoon fennel seeds

20 g (¾ oz) red onion, thinly sliced

60 g (2¼ oz) fennel bulb, thinly sliced

200 g (7 oz) strong bread (00) flour, approximately, plus extra for dusting

1½ teaspoon sea salt flakes

2 teaspoons freshly ground black pepper

To make the liver parfait, heat the oil in a heavy-based frying pan over medium heat. Add the onion and cook for 6–8 minutes or until just golden. Add the livers and cook for 3 minutes or until golden all over but still medium-rare in the middle. Add the brandy and carefully ignite the alcohol by tilting the pan towards the flame, if cooking over a gas flame, or use a lighter. When the flames have died down, stir in 100 g (3½ oz) of the butter and remove from the heat. Stand for 10 minutes, then stir in the vincotto and season to taste with sea salt and freshly ground black pepper. Transfer the mixture to a food processor and process until smooth. Push the mixture through a fine sieve, then transfer to a 500 ml (17 fl oz/2 cup) capacity shallow bowl and smooth the top. Cool a little. Meanwhile, melt the remaining butter, allow to cool, then pour over the parfait to seal. Cover with plastic wrap and refrigerate overnight.

To make the fennel bread, place the milk, sugar, yeast and 1 teaspoon of the oil in a large bowl and stand in a warm place for 10 minutes or until foamy.

Meanwhile, heat the remaining oil in a frying pan over low–medium heat. Add the fennel seeds and cook for 30 seconds or until fragrant. Add the onion and cook for 5–6 minutes or until translucent. Remove from the heat, stir in the sliced fennel and allow to cool. Set aside.

Once the yeast has activated, add the flour and salt, turn out onto a lightly floured surface and knead until a smooth dough forms. (You may need to a little more flour if it's too sticky.) Place the dough in a lightly oiled bowl, cover with a tea towel and stand in a warm, draught-free place for 45 minutes or until doubled in size.

Knead the cooled fennel mixture into the dough until evenly distributed — the dough will look quite rough. Shape the dough into a log and place on a baking tray lined with baking paper. Sprinkle with the pepper, then cover loosely with a tea towel and stand for another 15 minutes or until doubled in size.

Once risen, pick up the baking paper and dough and place in a large bamboo steamer basket placed over a saucepan of simmering water. Cover and steam for 15–20 minutes or until the bread is soft and spongy and an inserted skewer comes out clean. Remove from the steamer and cool. (At this stage the bread can be wrapped in plastic wrap and frozen for up to 1 week. It is important to freeze the bread as soon as it has cooled to maintain its freshness.)

Preheat the oven to 240°C (475°F/Gas 8). Place the cooled bread on a heavy-based baking tray and bake for 7 minutes or until golden (if using frozen fennel bread,

defrost before baking). Place on a wire rack to cool slightly. Serve slices of the warm fennel bread with the liver parfait.

Note Fresh yeast is available from health food stores, Italian delis and bakeries.

salumi misti con ciabatta a modo mio
mixed plate of small goods with my ciabatta

makes 1 loaf / serves 6

slices of salumi (see Note)
extra virgin olive oil, for dipping

ciabatta bread
250 ml (9 fl oz/1 cup) sparkling
    mineral water, approximately
2 tablespoons caster (superfine)
    sugar
2 tablespoons duck fat, melted
10 g (¼ oz) fresh yeast
    (see Note, page 71),
    crumbled
500 g (1 lb 2 oz) strong bread (00)
    flour, plus extra for dusting
2 teaspoons fine sea salt

To make the ciabatta, place the mineral water, sugar and half the melted duck fat in a bowl and combine well. Add the yeast, combine well, then stand in a warm place until the mixture begins to foam. Once the yeast has activated, add the flour and salt and stir until the dough comes together. Turn the dough out onto a lightly floured surface and knead for 5 minutes or until most of the big lumps are gone and there are no flour pockets. It should still be quite rough in appearance. Shape the dough into a log. Place on a heavy-based baking tray and use a knife to make deep slashes in the top of the dough. Brush the top with a little of the remaining duck fat. Cover with a tea towel and stand in a warm, draught-free place for 25 minutes or until risen by half.

Preheat the oven to 170°C (325°F/Gas 3). Brush the loaf again with a little duck fat. Bake for 30 minutes or until golden, brushing the top regularly with the remaining duck fat. Remove from the oven and stand for 10 minutes on the tray.

Half an hour before the ciabatta is ready, remove all the salumi from the refrigerator and bring to room temperature so the real flavours of the meat can come through.

To serve, arrange the salumi on a large serving platter and serve with extra virgin olive oil for dipping and lots of thickly sliced hot ciabatta.

Note It's important to choose salumi with varying levels of fat content, sweetness and heat to make sure the small goods plate is balanced. Two slices of each variety per person should be ample.

trippa con patate
tripe with potatoes

serves 4

Place the oil in a deep heavy-based saucepan over medium heat. Add the onion and garlic and cook for 5 minutes or until the onion is translucent. Increase the heat to high, then add the tripe and cook until very lightly browned.

Add the tomato and chilli, bring to the boil, then reduce the heat to low and simmer for 2 hours. Add the potato and cook for another 45 minutes or until the tripe is very tender.

Remove and discard the chilli. Season to taste with sea salt and freshly ground black pepper, stir in the pecorino and simmer for another 10 minutes. Stir in the basil and butter. Ladle into bowls and serve with crusty bread.

50 ml (1¾ fl oz) olive oil
1 small onion, chopped
1 garlic clove, sliced
250 g (9 oz) honeycomb tripe, cut into finger-sized pieces
400 g (14 oz) tinned chopped tomatoes
½ long red chilli, seeds removed
1 desiree potato, peeled and cut into 1.5 cm (⅝ inch) cubes
35 g (1¼ oz) pecorino, cut into 1.5 cm (⅝ inch) cubes
5 basil leaves
40 g (1½ oz) butter, chopped
crusty bread, to serve

insalata di polpo con giardiniera
octopus salad with pickled vegetables

serves 4

Using a small sharp knife, remove the peel and white pith from the lemon, then segment and remove any pips. Place in a bowl with the extra virgin olive oil, oregano, garlic and tomato. Using your hands, squash all the ingredients together to release their juices. Season to taste with sea salt and freshly ground black pepper and set aside.

Separate the octopus head from the tentacles. Cut the tentacles into bite-sized pieces.

Heat the olive oil in a large heavy-based frying pan over high heat. Add the octopus and cook for 1 minute or until slightly coloured and just cooked. Add to the tomato mixture and toss to combine. Add the giardiniera, toss again and serve.

1 lemon
50 ml (1¾ fl oz) extra virgin olive oil
1½ tablespoons oregano leaves
2 small garlic cloves, thinly sliced
1 small ox heart tomato, peeled, seeds removed and chopped
1 small octopus (about 250 g/9 oz), cleaned
1 tablespoon olive oil
150 g (5½ oz) drained giardiniera (see page 24), chopped

vitello tonnato
veal with tuna

serves 4

1 veal fillet (about 1.5 kg/3 lb 5 oz)
80 ml (2½ fl oz/⅓ cup) olive oil
2 teaspoons sea salt flakes
2 tablespoons freshly ground
    black pepper
125 g (4½ oz/½ cup) good-quality
    mayonnaise
200 g (7 oz) tinned tuna in oil,
    drained and flaked
1 tablespoon coarsely chopped
    flat-leaf (Italian) parsley
freshly squeezed lemon juice,
    to taste
extra virgin olive oil, for drizzling

Preheat the oven to 180°C (350°F/Gas 4).

Trim any sinew from the veal fillet. Using the muscle lines as a guide, separate all parts of the fillet at the butt end. Heat the olive oil in a large heavy-based frying pan over high heat. Cook the veal pieces until browned all over, then remove from the pan.

Place the salt and pepper on a plate and mix to combine. Roll the veal in the mixture to coat all over. Place on a baking tray and roast for 12 minutes. Remove from the oven and stand until cool.

Meanwhile, place the mayonnaise, tuna and parsley in a bowl. Season to taste with some lemon juice, salt and pepper and combine well.

Thinly slice the veal and arrange on a platter. Drizzle with a little extra virgin olive oil and serve with the tuna mayonnaise.

scaloppine farcite con provolone
stuffed veal escalopes filled with provolone

serves 4

Cut the provolone into eight 5 cm (2 inch) long, 1 cm (½ inch) thick slices. Finely grate the remainder.

Lay out the veal on a work surface and, using the flat side of a meat mallet, beat out until 3 mm (⅛ inch) thick all over. Season well with sea salt and freshly ground black pepper and sprinkle with half of the parsley. Place a slice of provolone at one end, roll up tightly and secure with toothpicks.

Place the oil in a shallow dish, add the rolled veal, turn gently to coat, then refrigerate the veal for 30 minutes.

Combine the grated provolone, breadcrumbs and remaining parsley in a shallow dish.

Remove the veal from the oil and reserve the oil. Working with one piece of veal at a time, pat the breadcrumb mixture on to coat well.

Heat the reserved oil in a large heavy-based frying pan over medium–high heat. Cook the veal for 4 minutes each side or until golden and crisp all over. Remove from the pan and rest for 4–5 minutes. Serve with lemon wedges.

150 g (5½ oz) provolone
8 veal escalopes (about 60 g/ 2¼ oz each) (ask an Italian butcher for these)
1 small handful flat-leaf (Italian) parsley leaves, coarsely chopped
90 ml (3 fl oz) olive oil
120 g (4¼ oz/1½ cups) fresh breadcrumbs
lemon wedges, to serve

fregola con triglia e cardi
cockles & red mullet with fregola

serves 4

60 ml (2 fl oz/¼ cup) olive oil
1 garlic clove, sliced
2 tablespoons finely chopped
    onion
100 g (3½ oz) cockles or clams
    (vongole), rinsed well
1 small tomato, peeled and
    chopped
250 ml (9 fl oz/1 cup) fish stock
    (see page 265)
45 g (1¾ oz) fregola (see Note)
8 basil leaves
100 g (3½ oz) red mullet fillets
extra virgin olive oil, for drizzling

Heat 2 tablespoons of the olive oil in a heavy-based saucepan over high heat. Add the garlic and onion and cook for 3–4 minutes or until the garlic caramelises and the onion is translucent.

Add the cockles and tomato and bring to a simmer. Add the stock, return to a simmer and season to taste with sea salt and freshly ground black pepper. Stir in the fregola and basil, remove from the heat, cover with a tight-fitting lid and stand for 8 minutes.

Season the red mullet fillets to taste. Heat the remaining olive oil in a large heavy-based frying pan and cook the fillets, skin-side down, until just golden. Turn and cook for another 1–2 minutes or until just cooked through. Place the fillets in a large shallow serving bowl, pour the cockle mixture over, drizzle with extra virgin olive oil and serve.

Note Fregola is a small pea-shaped pasta from Sardinia. If unavailable, substitute with Israeli couscous.

soppressata
brawn

serves 8

1 star anise

1 cinnamon stick

1 tablespoon white peppercorns

3 cloves

1 tablespoon brown mustard seeds

1 teaspoon coriander seeds

1 large onion, chopped

5 garlic cloves

4 field mushrooms, sliced

½ bunch flat-leaf (Italian)
    parsley stalks

1 large pig's trotter

1 large pig's cheek

2 pork shanks

150 g (5½ oz) pork skin

crisp salad and crusty bread,
    to serve

Place all the spices in a small frying pan over low heat and dry-fry until fragrant. Remove from the heat and place in a large saucepan or stockpot. Add the onion, garlic, mushrooms, parsley stalks and 5 litres (175 fl oz) water and bring to the boil, then reduce the heat to low and simmer for 3 hours. Strain and discard the solids. Set the stock aside.

Place the trotter, cheek, shanks and pork skin in a large saucepan or stockpot and add enough stock to cover. Simmer over very low heat for 12 hours or until the meat falls off the bone and the skin is falling apart. During cooking you will need to skim the fat and any other impurities from the surface and top up with extra stock or water when necessary to keep the meat covered. Remove from the heat, allow the meat to cool in the liquid, then refrigerate overnight.

The following day, remove any fat from the surface of the liquid. Gently reheat, then remove all the meat and pork skin from the pan and discard the bones. Roughly chop the meat and skin and return to the pan. Season to taste with sea salt and freshly ground black pepper, remove from the heat and allow the mixture to cool. Stir the mixture to make sure all the meat is evenly distributed, then pour into a 750 ml (26 fl oz/3 cup) capacity terrine mould, cover with plastic wrap and refrigerate overnight.

To serve, unmould the terrine, then thinly slice and serve with a crisp salad and crusty bread.

zamponi
stuffed pig's trotters

serves 6–8

Place the trotters in a dish, sprinkle over the salt and refrigerate for 5 hours.

Meanwhile, place the minced pork, wine and chilli in a bowl. Season to taste with sea salt and freshly ground black pepper and combine well. Cover and refrigerate for 45 minutes.

Heat 2 tablespoons of the olive oil in a frying pan over medium heat. Add the speck and cook until coloured but not crisp. Add the sage and cook for another 2–3 minutes or until fragrant. Remove from the heat and cool completely. Add to the chilled pork mixture and combine well. Rinse the trotters and pat dry. Stuff the pork and speck mixture into the trotter cavities. Using a large butcher's needle and kitchen string, sew up the trotters, making sure all the stuffing is secure.

Heat the remaining olive oil in a heavy-based saucepan, just large enough to fit the trotters snugly, over medium–high heat. Cook the trotters until browned all over, then remove from the pan. Add the Napoletana sauce and 300 ml (10½ fl oz) water to the pan and bring to a simmer. Return the trotters to the pan, cover and reduce the heat to as low as possible. Cook for 8 hours or until tender. Turn occasionally and top up with a little extra water when necessary to keep the trotters covered.

Remove the trotters from the sauce and allow to cool. Reserve the sauce in the pan. Cut the trotters crossways into 1 cm (½ inch) thick slices. Reheat the sauce over low heat, season to taste, return the trotter slices to the pan and cook until just warmed through. Spoon the sauce onto serving plates, top with the trotter slices and drizzle with a little extra virgin olive oil to serve.

2 large pig's trotters, bones removed (ask your kind butcher to do this)
105 g (3¾ oz) sea salt flakes
250 g (9 oz) minced (ground) pork (ask your butcher for a 60% meat to 40% fat ratio on a 1 cm/½ inch grind)
60 ml (2 fl oz/¼ cup) red wine
1 long red chilli, seeds removed and finely chopped
100 ml (3½ fl oz) olive oil
250 g (9 oz) speck, with skin on, diced
6 sage leaves, thinly sliced
300 ml (10½ fl oz) Napoletana sauce (see page 262)
extra virgin olive oil, for drizzling

il cotechino di capodanno
cotechino with lentils

serves 8

Preheat the oven to 130°C (250°F/Gas 1).

Heat the olive oil in a large heavy-based ovenproof saucepan over medium heat. Cook the ribs, in batches, until browned all over, then remove from the pan and set aside.

Add the onion, carrot, leek, celery and garlic and cook for 5 minutes or until softened. Add the lentils and combine well. Add the wine and deglaze the pan, scraping the base with a wooden spoon to remove any cooked-on pieces. Simmer until reduced by two-thirds.

Return the ribs to the pan, add the tomato and stock and return to a simmer. Add the cotechino, cover and bake for 4 hours or until the meat is falling off the bone.

Remove the cotechino from the pan and keep warm. Remove the ribs from the pan, discard the bones and coarsely chop the meat. Return the chopped meat to the pan. Place over medium heat and bring to a simmer. Skim any excess fat from the top, stir through the parsley and season to taste with sea salt and freshly ground black pepper.

To serve, divide the lentil mixture among shallow bowls. Slice the cotechino and place on top, then drizzle with extra virgin olive oil.

80 ml (2½ fl oz/⅓ cup) olive oil
16 meaty, fatty pork ribs
1 small onion, diced
1 small carrot, diced
1 small leek, white part only, diced
1 small stalk celery, diced
1 garlic clove, chopped
200 g (7 oz) Puy (tiny blue-green) lentils
125 ml (4 fl oz/½ cup) red wine
400 g (14 oz) tinned chopped tomatoes
500 ml (17 fl oz/2 cups) veal stock (see page 264)
1 large cotechino (about 750 g/ 1 lb 10 oz)
1 small handful flat-leaf (Italian) parsley leaves, chopped
extra virgin olive oil, for drizzling

fegatini di anatra con pera e cavolo nero
duck liver with pear compote & cavolo nero

serves 4

300 g (10½ oz) desiree potatoes
(about 4 small)
300 ml (10½ fl oz) duck fat
60 ml (2 fl oz/¼ cup) olive oil
½ long red chilli, seeds removed
and finely chopped
1 garlic clove, finely chopped
1 bunch cavolo nero (Tuscan
black kale) (about 140 g/5 oz),
stalks trimmed, cut into 2 cm
(¾ inch) pieces
150 g (5½ oz) cleaned duck livers,
trimmed
2 small French shallots,
finely chopped
1½ tablespoons sherry vinegar
50 g (1¾ oz) butter, chopped

pear compote
½ lemon
200 g (7 oz) beurre bosc pear
(about 1 large)
50 g (1¾ oz) brown sugar
2 tablespoons balsamic vinegar

To make the pear compote, fill a bowl with water, squeeze the lemon into the water, then add the lemon half. Peel and core the pear. Cut the pear into 1 cm (½ inch) cubes, placing them in the acidulated water as you go. Drain the pears, then place in a small heavy-based saucepan with the sugar over low heat. Stir for 3 minutes or until all the sugar is dissolved. Add the vinegar, increase the heat to medium and simmer for 25–30 minutes or until thickened and reduced but still chunky. Remove from the heat and set aside.

Preheat the oven to 120°C (235°F/Gas ½). Peel the potatoes, then, using a mandolin or large sharp knife, cut into thin rounds. Pat dry with a tea towel. Heat the duck fat in a small deep saucepan to 150°C (300°F). Fry the potato, in batches, turning once, until golden and crisp. Drain on absorbent paper and keep warm in the oven until ready to serve.

Heat half of the oil in a large frying pan over medium heat. Add the chilli and garlic and cook for 1–2 minutes or until the garlic is translucent. Add the cavolo nero, toss to combine and cook for another 2–3 minutes or until just wilted. Season to taste with sea salt and freshly ground black pepper. Remove from the heat and keep warm.

Meanwhile, heat the remaining oil in another large heavy-based frying pan over high heat. Add the livers and toss for 1–2 minutes or until golden all over but still rare in the middle. Add the shallot and vinegar, simmer for 30 seconds, then season to taste and stir in the butter.

To serve, top the cavolo nero with the livers and potato slices. Serve with the pear on the side.

uova strapazzate con patate
fried potatoes
with eggs & pecorino

serves 8

Peel the potatoes and cut into 2 cm (¾ inch) cubes. Drop the potato into a saucepan of lightly salted boiling water and cook for 3 minutes or until just tender but still firm to the bite. Drain well, then allow to cool.

Melt the butter in a heavy-based frying pan over medium heat. Add the garlic and cook for 2 minutes or until caramelised. Add the potato and cook until golden all over. Pour the beaten egg over the potato and stir gently with a wooden spoon to just combine. Add the pecorino and parsley and season to taste with sea salt and freshly ground black pepper. Slowly stir until the mixture is scrambled. As soon as it is beginning to set, but still wet, stir one last time, then transfer to a plate and enjoy with toasted bread.

400 g (14 oz) desiree potatoes
20 g (¾ oz) butter
3 garlic cloves, crushed
4 eggs, lightly beaten
150 g (5½ oz/1⅔ cups) finely
    grated pecorino
1 small handful flat-leaf (Italian)
    parsley leaves, chopped
toasted bread, to serve

insalate
salads with gusto

My mum always says the more interesting the salad, the more it's eaten. In an Italian household, salad is more than just leaves — it usually consists of any leftovers lightened up with a dressing and served in a completely different guise to the original. This resourcefulness is at the heart of Italian cooking: nothing is disposed of, it's just served in another form, so one dish can transform into 10 others.

Growing up, I always had the following salads as lunchtime snacks. They're not your typical lettuce-and-tomato numbers but they're what my parents called salads. Right or wrong, I still make them to this day and they inspire me to mix and match new flavours to use up leftovers.

insalata caprese
tomato & buffalo mozzarella salad
serves 6

Thinly slice the tomatoes, arrange on a plate and top with the basil. Slice each mozzarella ball into 3–4 pieces. Arrange on top of the tomato. Drizzle generously with the oil and season to taste with sea salt and freshly ground black pepper.

6 ripe small ox heart tomatoes
12 basil leaves
2 buffalo mozzarella balls
    (about 180 g/6½ oz each),
    at room temperature
extra virgin olive oil, for drizzling

insalata di broccolini
broccolini salad
serves 4–6

Heat the oil in a large frying pan over medium heat. Add the garlic and cook until just golden, then add the onion and cook for another 4–5 minutes or until the onion is caramelised. Add the chilli and combine well.

Increase the heat to high, add the broccolini to the pan, then the wine and vinegar, combine well, cover and allow to sizzle for about 4–5 minutes or until the broccolini is just tender. Remove from the heat and cool to room temperature. Season to taste with sea salt and freshly ground black pepper and serve.

2 tablespoons olive oil
2 garlic cloves, thinly sliced
1½ tablespoons finely chopped
    onion
2 teaspoons confit red chilli
    (see page 263) or
    ½ long red chilli, seeds
    removed and finely chopped
3 bunches broccolini, roughly
    chopped
2 tablespoons red wine
2 tablespoons red wine vinegar

insalata di maiale
pork salad

serves 6

60 ml (2 fl oz/¼ cup) olive oil
300 g (10½ oz) minced (ground)
  pork (ask your butcher for
  an 80% meat to 20% fat ratio
  on a 1 cm/½ inch grind)
1 onion, thinly sliced
2 confit garlic cloves
  (see page 263), finely chopped
1 medium handful flat-leaf (Italian)
  parsley leaves, chopped
juice of 2 small lemons
1½ tablespoons extra virgin
  olive oil
6 thin prosciutto slices
lemon cheeks and crusty bread,
  to serve

Heat the olive oil in a large frying pan over medium–high heat. Add the pork and cook, breaking up any lumps with the back of a wooden spoon, until well browned and slightly crisp. Remove the pork with a slotted spoon and place in a large bowl.

Add the onion to the pan, reduce the heat to medium and cook for 5 minutes or until caramelised. Add to the pork along with the confit garlic and toss to combine.

Add the parsley, lemon juice and extra virgin olive oil to the pork mixture. Season to taste with sea salt and freshly ground black pepper and toss gently to combine. Transfer to a large platter and allow to cool.

Lay the prosciutto slices on top and serve with the lemon cheeks and crusty bread.

insalata di radicchio
radicchio salad

serves 4

Wash the radicchio and herbs and drain well. Place in a bowl and toss together using your hands to combine. Crumble the ricotta infornata over the radicchio, add the pecorino and toss very gently. Drizzle over the vinegar, then the oil, season to taste with sea salt and freshly ground black pepper and toss again. Place on a large plate or shallow bowl and serve immediately.

1 head radicchio, leaves separated and outer ones discarded
10 mint leaves
10 basil leaves
75 g (2¾ oz) ricotta infornata (see page 23)
2 tablespoons shaved pecorino
1½ tablespoons aged balsamic vinegar
1½ tablespoons extra virgin olive oil

insalata di finocchio e gorgonzola
gorgonzola & fennel salad

serves 6

2 tablespoons olive oil
4 thin Italian sausages
2 bulbs baby fennel
2 tablespoons extra virgin olive oil
2 tablespoons white wine vinegar
110 g (3¾ oz) Gorgonzola
    Dolcelatte

Heat half of the olive oil in a frying pan over medium heat. Add the sausages and cook until golden all over but not cooked through. Remove from the pan and allow to cool, then halve lengthways.

Heat the remaining oil in the same pan, return the sausages to the pan and cook for 2 minutes both sides or until golden and cooked through. Remove from the heat and cool slightly.

Remove the tough outer layers and core of the fennel bulbs and discard. Using a mandolin or large sharp knife, shave the fennel into matchsticks. Place in a bowl, add the extra virgin olive oil and vinegar, season to taste with sea salt and freshly ground black pepper and toss to combine well.

Place the fennel on a large heatproof serving plate, top with the sausage halves and crumble the Gorgonzola all over. Place under a hot grill (broiler) for 10 seconds or until the cheese is slightly melted. Serve immediately.

insalata di osso buco
osso buco salad

serves 8

Preheat the oven to 170ºC (325ºF/Gas 3).

Heat the oil in a large heavy-based ovenproof saucepan over high heat. Cook the osso buco, in batches, and cook until browned on both sides. Remove from the pan and set aside.

Add the onion, carrot and celery to the pan and stir for 5 minutes or until lightly coloured. Return the meat to the pan, add the tomato and stock and bring to the boil. Cover and bake for 3 hours or until the meat is meltingly tender.

Remove the osso buco from the pan. When cool enough to handle, remove the meat and marrow from the bones and set aside. Discard the bones.

Place the pan over medium heat, add the basil and simmer until the sauce is reduced by half. Return the meat and marrow to the pan, add the citrus rind, bring to a simmer, then remove from the heat. Allow to cool, then refrigerate overnight.

Add the vinegar to the meat, season to taste with sea salt and freshly ground black pepper and combine well. Place on a serving plate and serve with the sliced egg and crusty bread.

60 ml (2 fl oz/¼ cup) olive oil
8 pieces osso buco (centre cut only)
1 onion, diced
1 small carrot, diced
1 small stalk celery, diced
400 g (14 oz) tinned chopped tomatoes
400 ml (14 fl oz) chicken stock (see page 264)
10 basil leaves
2 wide strips lemon rind, white pith removed, thinly sliced
2 wide strips orange rind, white pith removed, thinly sliced
80 ml (2½ fl oz/⅓ cup) red wine vinegar
3 eggs, hard-boiled, peeled and sliced
crusty bread, to serve

the perpetual garden

When my family moved to Australia, my parents grew lots of vegetables as was the custom of the small community of Italians they lived among. We had two or three fruit trees, an olive tree, and grew green salad leaves and every kind of bean. Even though there was a great community spirit, Italians are quite competitive by nature and those who grew the best crop each season would be very protective of their prize-winning harvest; they would share their seeds and graft plants with only a chosen few… But my dad always found interesting ways to befriend the right family to secure a bag of the best seeds for our garden.

There was always lots of activity going on and I learnt from a very early age about only eating produce in season. The first and second pickings of any harvest would be tender and sweet, so we ate them on their own or with very little else. The third and fourth pickings weren't as sweet but still delicate, so we would make them into something quick and simple. Pickings after that were best suited for cooking, stewing or roasting rather than eating fresh. And we always saved the seeds from the last harvest for the next year's planting.

My mum has given up her gardening days, but she still grows wild asparagus and uses them to make an amazing frittata. In a typical Italian garden you'll find the following…

chilli Australians don't seem to take advantage of the many types of chillies (peppers) available. Spring chilli suits lighter dishes, such as spring lamb and spring onion (scallions), while winter chilli suits root vegetables and richer roasts.

eggplant Tender white eggplants (aubergines) are only available for a short season, making them such a luxury. Cook them in pasta or grill them on their own and eat them hot. Purple eggplants, which are a little tougher but still delicious, are better baked or pickled.

beetroot Roasted beets are great in salads and I always had them this way as a kid. When we arrived in Australia, my mum came across the classic can of beets pickled in their own juices, and she loved the idea so much that she started pickling her own.

zucchini It's quite trendy these days to see fragile zucchini (courgette) flowers from the young vegetable on restaurant menus. I remember eating them as a kid, lightly floured, then quickly fried. The second harvest of zucchinis are great boiled quickly and served simply, and the last harvest is best fried, pickled or marinated.

beans We had so many varieties of beans in the garden. Fresh beans are so different from the dried version you see in supermarkets. All they need is a quick blanch to really appreciate their flavour. Just-picked broad (fava) beans don't need to be cooked, but can be eaten straight in their pods with their shells on. Older broad beans which need to be podded and peeled are better cooked — my family's favourite way is to make them into a purée for bruschetta.

bitter leaves This is what my mum and dad call 'medicine food'. Growing up, we would eat bitter greens at least once a week to cleanse the body. We had many different types — cavolo nero (Tuscan black kale), cime di rape (turnip greens), all varieties of endive and chard.

insalata di polpo marinato
marinated octopus salad

serves 6

700 g (1 lb 9 oz) cleaned octopus
100 ml (3½ fl oz) olive oil
3 garlic cloves, sliced
400 g (14 oz) tinned chopped
    tomatoes
1 medium handful flat-leaf (Italian)
    parsley leaves, chopped
crusty bread and lemon cheeks,
    to serve

Cut the octopus tentacles and head into 2.5 cm (1 inch) pieces.

Heat the oil and garlic in a large heavy-based frying pan over high heat and cook for 2 minutes or until caramelised. Add the octopus and cook for 10 minutes or until all the liquid has been released from the octopus.

Add the tomato and parsley, reduce the heat to low and simmer for 30–40 minutes or until the sauce is reduced by one-third, the oil begins to rise to the top and the octopus is tender. Remove from the heat, season to taste with sea salt and freshly ground black pepper and cool. Serve with the crusty bread and lemon cheeks.

insalata di acciughe e uova
egg & marinated anchovy salad

serves 4

Place the anchovies on a large serving plate and scatter over the basil.

Butter both sides of the bread slices with the extra butter, then cook in a large non-stick frying pan over medium heat until golden on both sides. Remove from the pan and keep warm.

Add the butter to the pan and fry the eggs, sunny side up, until just cooked but still runny in the middle. Remove from the heat, place the eggs on top of the anchovies, then coarsely tear the bread over the top and serve immediately.

Note White anchovies are available from good Italian or Spanish delis.

16 white anchovies marinated
  in oil (see Note), drained
16 basil leaves, torn
4 slices ciabatta bread
  (see page 74)
40 g (1½ oz) butter, softened,
  plus extra for spreading
4 eggs

terrina di lattuga romana e trota affumicata
smoked trout & cos lettuce pressed salad

serves 6–8

4 baby cos (romaine) lettuces,
    outer leaves discarded
80 ml (2½ fl oz/⅓ cup) white wine
    vinegar
60 ml (2 fl oz/¼ cup) extra
    virgin olive oil, plus extra
    for drizzling
150 g (5½ oz) smoked trout,
    flesh flaked, skin and
    bones removed
lemon wedges, to serve

Separate and wash the lettuce leaves and place in a large bowl. Add the vinegar, oil and flaked trout. Toss together and season to taste with sea salt and freshly ground black pepper, keeping in mind that the trout has a salty taste.

Place in a 21 x 9 x 5 cm (8 x 3.5 x 2 inch) terrine mould or tin lined with plastic wrap, cover with extra wrap and place a heavy weight, such as food tins, on top. Refrigerate overnight.

To serve, drain the juices, then turn out the terrine onto a chopping board. Using a large sharp knife, cut into slices, place on serving plates, drizzle with a little oil and serve with the lemon wedges.

insalata di baccalà
salt cod salad with chilli

serves 6

Drain and pat dry the salt cod. Place the stock in a saucepan, bring to a simmer, then add the salt cod and simmer very gently for 20 minutes. Drain, remove any skin and bones from the salt cod and discard. Flake the flesh into a bowl.

Meanwhile, heat the olive oil in a large frying pan over medium–high heat. Season the blue-eye to taste with sea salt and freshly ground black pepper and cook each side until golden and just cooked through. Remove from the heat, cool and flake into the bowl with the salt cod.

Add the confit chilli, mint, lemon juice and extra virgin olive oil, season to taste and toss gently to combine. Toss through the giardiniera and serve scattered with the pecorino.

Note Salt cod is a traditional method of preserving cod in salt. The salt draws out the moisture in the flesh, resulting in a richer, deeper flavour than the fresh version. You can buy it at Italian grocers and delis.

300 g (10½ oz) salt cod, soaked in water for 48 hours, water changed 4 times (see Note)

750 ml (26 fl oz/3 cups) vegetable stock (see page 265)

1 tablespoon olive oil

150 g (5½ oz) blue-eye trevalla fillet

1 tablespoon confit green chilli (see page 263)

6 mint leaves, torn

juice of 1 lemon

60 ml (2 fl oz/¼ cup) extra virgin olive oil

120 g (4¼ oz) drained giardiniera (see page 24)

70 g (2½ oz) pecorino, shaved

insalata di agrumi ed olive
blood orange & olive salad

serves 4

4 oranges
3 blood oranges
100 g (3½ oz) drained olive
    schiacciate (see page 30)
2 tablespoons olive oil
1 long red chilli, halved and
    seeds removed

Using a small sharp knife, remove the rind from the oranges, then remove any bitter white pith. Segment the oranges, making sure there are no seeds or pith. Arrange on a serving plate and scatter over the olive schiacciate.

Just before serving, place the oil and chilli in a small frying pan over low heat. Cook until the chilli just starts to soften and blister, then pour the hot oil and chilli over the oranges. Season to taste with sea salt and freshly ground black pepper and serve immediately.

caponatina con manzo
beef & caponatina

serves 6

Cut the eggplant, zucchini, onion, tomatoes and olives into 1 cm (½ inch) cubes and keep separate.

Heat 2 cm (¾ inch) of oil in a large heavy-based frying pan over medium–high heat. Cook the eggplant, zucchini and onion, separately until golden. When each vegetable is cooked, pour into a sieve placed over a bowl, return the oil to the pan and continue cooking the remaining vegetables. Once the last vegetable is cooked, return the oil to the pan again, add the garlic and cook until just golden. Add the garlic to the vegetables and reserve any oil in the pan for tossing through the salad later.

Fill a small deep saucepan one-third full with fresh oil and place over medium heat. When the oil reaches 150°C (300°F) or until a cube of bread dropped into the oil browns in 25 seconds, deep-fry the parsley for 30 seconds or until translucent, being careful as the oil will spit. Remove with a slotted spoon and drain on absorbent paper. Repeat with the basil.

Place the vegetable mixture, fried herbs, tomato, olives and pine nuts in a large bowl and toss together gently. Add the vinegar and just enough reserved oil to coat the vegetables. Season to taste with sea salt and freshly ground black pepper, toss gently to combine and place on a large serving plate. Set aside.

Heat a char-grill pan or barbecue flatplate to high. Lightly brush the beef with a little of the reserved oil and season to taste. Cook for 3 minutes each side for medium-rare or until cooked to your liking. Rest in a warm place for 5 minutes, then thinly slice. Place on top of the caponatina and serve.

1 eggplant (aubergine)
1 zucchini (courgette)
1 white onion
2 ox heart tomatoes, peeled
12 jumbo green olives, pitted
olive oil, for shallow-frying
2 garlic cloves, thinly sliced
1 medium handful flat-leaf (Italian) parsley leaves, chopped
1 medium handful basil leaves
100 g (3½ oz) pine nuts, toasted
80 ml (2½ fl oz/⅓ cup) red wine vinegar
2 pieces centre-cut beef fillet (about 150 g/5½ oz each)

bruschetta calabrese
tomato & toasted bread salad

serves 6

Preheat the oven to 180°C (350°F/Gas 4).

Halve the ciabatta lengthways and rub the cut sides with the garlic. Cut the bread into 2 cm (¾ inch) pieces, place on a baking tray and bake for 20 minutes or until crisp and golden. Place in a bowl and set aside.

Chop the tomatoes into 1 cm (½ inch) cubes. Place in a bowl with the oil and mineral water and season to taste with sea salt and freshly ground black pepper. Mix through using your fingertips to combine well.

Just before serving, add the tomato dressing to the bread and toss to combine. Serve immediately before the bread becomes soggy.

½ loaf stale ciabatta bread
  (see page 74)
1 garlic clove
2 ox heart tomatoes
60 ml (2 fl oz/¼ cup) extra virgin
  olive oil
60–80 ml (2–2½ fl oz/¼–⅓ cup)
  sparkling mineral water,
  for drizzling

fagioli in pomodoro con tonno annerito
tuna & bean salad

serves 6

1 tablespoon olive oil
1 white onion, thinly sliced
3 garlic cloves, thinly sliced
400 g (14 oz) tinned chopped
tomatoes
350 g (12 oz) snake (yard-long)
or green beans, cut into 5 cm
(2 inch) lengths
1½ tablespoons sea salt flakes
1 tablespoon coarsely ground
black pepper
300 g (10½ oz) cannon of tuna
(ask your fishmonger for this)

Heat the oil in a heavy-based saucepan over low heat. Add the onion and garlic and cook for 5 minutes or until the garlic is caramelised. Add the tomato and bring to a simmer. Add the beans, cover and simmer for 45 minutes or until the fragrance of the beans come through. Remove from the heat, season with sea salt and freshly ground black pepper and cool to room temperature.

Meanwhile, place the salt and pepper on a large plate and combine well. Roll the tuna in the mixture until well coated all over.

Heat a large non-stick frying pan over high heat. When it is very hot, add the tuna and cook for 1 minute each side so it is still rare in the middle. Allow to cool, then refrigerate until chilled.

Cut the tuna into 5 mm (¼ inch) thick slices. Spread the beans over a large serving plate and top with the tuna.

brodi, polenta e risotti
italian comfort food

When I was feeling sick or blue as a child, my mum would always cook a broth to make me feel better. Today I cook these for my children and they have the same reaction I did when I was young. In my household, I always find that food is a way of solving any problem. If there was any leftover brodo, my mum would use it in a risotto or polenta in addition to stock for extra flavour.

Polenta is a typical northern Italian dish and eaten in place of pasta, rice and bread. It's served with warm, comforting dishes such as braises and casseroles. Big platters and bowls are usually placed in the centre of the table for communal eating with plenty of polenta to mop up the sauces.

brodo di pollo
chicken broth

serves 6

1 whole chicken (about 1.6 kg/
   3 lb 8 oz), excess fat trimmed
2 carrots
2 stalks celery
2 onions
⅓ bunch flat-leaf (Italian)
   parsley stalks
150 g (5½ oz) pastina (see Note)
finely grated pecorino, to serve

Place the chicken, vegetables and parsley stalks in a large heavy-based saucepan and add 3½–4 litres (122–140 fl oz) water or enough to cover well. Bring to the boil, then reduce the heat to low and simmer gently for 4 hours. Skim any scum from the surface regularly.

Remove the chicken from the pan. Strain the broth into a clean pan and reserve the vegetables. When cool enough to handle, remove and discard the skin and bones from the chicken, then cut the meat into finger-sized strips. Cut the vegetables into finger-sized pieces, too.

Return the broth to the boil, add the pastina, stir well and simmer until al dente. Return the chicken and vegetables to the pan, bring to the boil and season to taste with sea salt and freshly ground black pepper. Remove from the heat and stand for 5 minutes. Ladle into bowls and scatter with a good helping of pecorino.

Note Pastina is any small pasta usually used for soups. It's available from good Italian delis.

brodo di lenticchie
lentil broth

serves 6

Heat the olive oil in a large heavy-based saucepan over low–medium heat. Add the onion, carrot and celery and cook until softened but not browned. Add the lentils and stir for 5 minutes. Add the potato and stock, bring to the boil, then reduce the heat to low and simmer for 1–1½ hours or until tender. Skim any scum from the surface regularly.

Add the pastina, stir well and simmer until al dente. Season to taste with sea salt and freshly ground black pepper, remove from the heat and stand for 5 minutes.

Meanwhile, heat the butter in a large frying pan over medium–high heat. When foaming but not brown, add the bread and stir until golden and crisp all over. Season to taste with pepper.

Ladle the broth into bowls, top with the croutons and drizzle with extra virgin olive oil to serve.

60 ml (2 fl oz/¼ cup) olive oil
2 onions, finely chopped
1 carrot, finely chopped
1 small stalk celery, finely chopped
200 g (7 oz) Puy (tiny blue-green) lentils
2 desiree potatoes, finely chopped
2.5 litres (87 fl oz) vegetable stock (see page 265)
100 g (3½ oz) pastina (see Note, opposite)
100 g (3½ oz) butter, chopped
¼ loaf ciabatta bread (see page 74), torn into small pieces
extra virgin olive oil, for drizzling

brodo di ceci
chickpea broth

serves 6

Heat the olive oil in a large heavy-based saucepan over medium heat. Add the onion, celery, leek, carrot and potato and cook for 6–8 minutes or until softened but not browned.

Add the chickpeas and stock and bring to a simmer. Reduce the heat to low and cook for 2½–3 hours or until the chickpeas are tender. Skim any scum from the surface regularly.

Add the pastina, stir well and simmer until al dente. Season to taste with sea salt and freshly ground black pepper. Ladle into bowls and top with a few pieces of the torn mozzarella and ciabatta for soaking up the broth. Drizzle with the extra virgin olive oil to serve.

Note Pastina is any small pasta usually used for soups. It's available from good Italian delis.

60 ml (2 fl oz/¼ cup) olive oil
2 onions, finely chopped
1 small stalk celery, finely chopped
1 leek, white part only, finely chopped
1 carrot, finely chopped
2 desiree potatoes, finely chopped
200 g (7 oz) chickpeas, soaked overnight in water, drained
2.5 litres (87 fl oz) chicken stock (see page 264)
100 g (3½ oz) pastina (see Note)
2 buffalo mozzarella balls, torn
½ loaf ciabatta bread (see page 74), torn into large pieces
extra virgin olive oil, for drizzling

brodo di fave
broad bean broth

serves 6

60 ml (2 fl oz/¼ cup) olive oil
2 onions, finely chopped
1 leek, white part only,
    finely chopped
3 desiree potatoes, finely chopped
1.2 kg (2 lb 10 oz) fresh broad
    (fava) beans, podded and
    peeled (or 700 g/1 lb 9 oz
    frozen, peeled)
2.5 litres (87 fl oz) vegetable
    stock (see page 265)
100 g (3½ oz) pastina (see Note)
extra virgin olive oil, for drizzling

Heat the olive oil in a large heavy-based saucepan over medium heat. Add the onion, leek and potato and cook for 6–8 minutes or until softened but not browned. Add the peeled broad beans and stock and simmer for 4 hours. By this time, the broad beans will have broken down and thickened the broth.

Season to taste with sea salt and freshly ground black pepper. Add the pastina, stir well and simmer until al dente. Ladle into bowls, drizzle over a little of the extra virgin olive oil and grind over black pepper to serve.

Note Pastina is any small pasta usually used for soups. It's available from good Italian delis.

brodo di patate e pancetta
potato & pork belly broth

serves 6

Heat the olive oil in a heavy-based saucepan over medium heat. Add the onion and pork belly and cook for 8–10 minutes or until the onion is just beginning to brown. Add the garlic and cook until the garlic is just lightly browned.

Add the potato and cook for another 5 minutes. Add the tomato and stock and bring to a simmer. Reduce the heat to low and simmer for 3 hours or until the pork is tender and falling apart.

Season to taste with sea salt and freshly ground black pepper. Add the pastina, stir well and simmer until al dente. Ladle into bowls, drizzle over a little of the extra virgin olive oil and serve with slices of the ciabatta on the side.

Note Pastina is any small pasta usually used for soups. It's available from good Italian delis.

60 ml (2 fl oz/¼ cup) olive oil
1 onion, thinly sliced
200 g (7 oz) boneless pork belly, skin on, cut into 3 cm (1¼ inch) pieces
3 garlic cloves, sliced
650 g (1 lb 7 oz) desiree potatoes, peeled and cut into 1 cm (½ inch) cubes
400 g (14 oz) tinned chopped tomatoes
1.5 litres (87 fl oz) chicken stock (see page 264)
100 g (3½ oz) pastina (see Note)
extra virgin olive oil, for drizzling
ciabatta bread (see page 74), to serve

zuppa di frattaglie con malfatti
offal soup with fresh pasta

serves 8

60 ml (2 fl oz/¼ cup) olive oil

1 large onion, finely chopped

2 garlic cloves, thinly sliced

2 pig's trotters, halved lengthways
(ask your butcher to do this)

150 g (5½ oz) beef cheek,
coarsely diced

2 litres (70 fl oz) chicken stock
(see page 264)

100 g (3½ oz) chicken liver,
trimmed and diced

150 g (5½ oz) lamb heart, diced

150 g (5½ oz) sweetbreads, diced

1 bunch cavolo nero (Tuscan
black kale), stems removed,
leaves coarsely chopped

200 g (7 oz) fresh pappardelle, cut
into 2 cm (¾ inch) long pieces

extra virgin olive oil, for drizzling

100 g (3½ oz/1 cup) finely grated
pecorino

toasted focaccia, to serve

Heat the olive oil in a heavy-based saucepan over medium heat. Add the onion and garlic and cook for 6–8 minutes or until translucent. Add the pig's trotters and beef cheek and cook until lightly coloured. Add the stock, bring to the boil, then reduce the heat to low and simmer for 2 hours, skimming the surface regularly.

Remove the trotters and, when cool enough to handle, remove and shred the meat and return to the broth.

Bring the broth back to a simmer. Add the liver, heart and sweetbreads and simmer for 3 minutes, then add the cavolo nero and pasta and simmer for another 3 minutes. Remove from the heat and season to taste with sea salt and freshly ground black pepper. Ladle into deep bowls, sprinkle with the pecorino and drizzle with the extra virgin olive oil. Serve with the toasted focaccia.

Polenta is great to mop up sauces, especially casserole sauces. Top the polenta with the sauce of your choice and finish with a drizzle of extra virgin olive oil. Grate over some parmesan or pecorino for meat-based dishes. Traditionally parmesan isn't paired with seafood so use poor man's parmesan (see page 263) for seafood-based sauces. Have your casserole or sauce nearly done before you start making the polenta. While the polenta is resting, you can add the finishing touches to your sauce, then serve while the polenta is still warm.

polenta forte
basic polenta

serves 4

Place the stock and butter in a large heavy-based saucepan over medium heat and season to taste with sea salt and freshly ground black pepper. Bring to a simmer, then, while whisking continuously, gradually pour in the polenta. Bring to a simmer again, then reduce the heat to low and cook, stirring continuously with a wooden spoon, for 30 minutes or until thickened.

Pour onto a large wooden board and allow to rest for 5 minutes before serving.

750 ml (26 fl oz/3 cups) vegetable stock (see page 265)
120 g (4¼ oz) butter, chopped
150 g (5½ oz/1 cup) coarse polenta

polenta con spezzatino di pollo
polenta with chicken casserole

serves 4

Heat 2 tablespoons of the oil in a large heavy-based saucepan over medium–high heat. Cook the chicken, in batches, until lightly browned all over, then remove from the pan.

Add the remaining oil to the pan, then add the onion, zucchini, olives, potato and garlic and cook for 8–10 minutes or until lightly coloured. Return the chicken to the pan, add the herbs, mustard seeds and peppercorns and combine well. Add the tomato and season to taste with sea salt and freshly ground black pepper. Cover, reduce the heat to as low as possible and simmer for 2 hours or until the chicken is succulent but not dry.

Serve the chicken and sauce on top of the polenta and scatter over a little of the poor man's parmesan.

60 ml (2 fl oz/¼ cup) olive oil
4 chicken drumsticks
4 chicken thighs, bone in, skin on
1 onion, sliced
1 large zucchini (courgette), finely chopped
45 g (1¾ oz/¼ cup) black olives
1 desiree potato, peeled and finely chopped
3 garlic cloves, thinly sliced
1 small handful flat-leaf (Italian) parsley leaves, chopped
1 small handful basil leaves
1 tablespoon brown mustard seeds
1 tablespoon drained green peppercorns in brine
400 g (14 oz) tinned chopped tomatoes
1 quantity basic polenta (see page 133)
poor man's parmesan (see page 263), to serve

polenta con dentice alla puttanesca
polenta with puttanesca snapper

serves 4

4 small snapper fillets
(about 120 g/4¼ oz each),
skin on
60 ml (2 fl oz/¼ cup) olive oil
1 onion, finely chopped
60 g (2¼ oz/½ cup) pitted
green olives
15 salted baby capers, rinsed
1 tablespoon confit red chilli
(see page 263)
5 anchovy fillets
⅓ cup coarsely chopped flat-leaf
(Italian) parsley leaves
400 g (14 oz) tinned chopped
tomatoes
1 quantity basic polenta
(see page 133)
poor man's parmesan
(see page 263), to serve

Season the snapper to taste with sea salt and freshly ground black pepper. Heat 2 tablespoons of the oil in a large frying pan over medium–high heat. Cook the snapper fillets, skin-side down, for 3 minutes, without moving or until crisp. Turn and cook for another 30 seconds. Remove from the pan, set aside and keep warm.

Reduce the heat to medium, add the remaining oil to the pan, then add the onion and cook for 5 minutes or until translucent. Add the olives, capers, confit chilli, anchovies and parsley and stir for 5 minutes or until fragrant. Add the tomato and simmer for 5 minutes or until the tomato starts to break down. Season to taste, then add the snapper and simmer until just heated through.

Serve the snapper and sauce on top of the polenta and scatter with the poor man's parmesan.

This is a great dish when earthy fresh mushrooms are in season. You must make sure you cook the mushrooms over high heat. If the temperature of the pan drops or is too low, the liquid in the mushrooms will escape and the mushrooms will braise instead of sauté and will be soggy instead of golden and crisp.

polenta con funghi trifolati
polenta with sautéed mushrooms

serves 4

Wipe any excess dirt from the mushrooms with a soft cloth or a soft-bristled brush. Cut any larger mushrooms down to the same size as the smaller mushrooms so they are all uniform in size.

Heat the oil in a large frying pan over high heat. When it just begins to smoke, immediately add the mushrooms. Cook, tossing, until golden and the liquid has evaporated, then add the garlic, onion and parsley and cook until the mushrooms start to crisp up. Season to taste with sea salt and freshly ground black pepper. Remove half of the mushrooms from the pan, set aside and keep warm.

Add the stock to the pan and simmer until reduced to a sauce-like consistency, then fold in the butter.

Pour the hot polenta onto a large wooden board and make a well in the centre. Pour the mushroom sauce into the well, place the reserved mushrooms on top and scatter over the poor man's parmesan.

100 g (3½ oz) fresh porcini (cep) mushrooms
100 g (3½ oz) fresh chanterelle mushrooms
30 g (1 oz) fresh morel mushrooms
100 g (3½ oz) button mushrooms
100 g (3½ oz) pine mushrooms
60 ml (2 fl oz/¼ cup) olive oil
3 garlic cloves, thinly sliced
1 onion, thinly sliced
1 small handful flat-leaf (Italian) parsley leaves, chopped
150 ml (5 fl oz) veal stock (see page 264)
40 g (1½ oz) butter, chopped
1 quantity basic polenta (see page 133)
poor man's parmesan (see page 263) or grated parmesan, to serve

risotto

There are a few golden rules to making risotto. First, to infuse flavour, cook the rice in stocks, as well as soups or purées. Second, risotto should never be served so steaming hot that your taste buds burn. Let it cool a little before serving to let the flavours of your ingredients really shine. And lastly, never serve a risotto as clumps of rice on a plate, as if you were building a house with cement.

the right rice

There are three types of rice used to make risotto: vialone nano, carnaroli and arborio, and each is used specifically with certain ingredients. If you want a superb product, it's important to use the right type of rice.

vialone nano These robust grains have high levels of starch, so they hold their shape well. It's perfect for strong flavours such as a rich ragù, meaty casseroles, braises, game and even flavoursome seafood using flathead and mussels (see page 147) or salted cod with tomato and capers.

carnaroli Balanced levels of starch and a daintier shape lend this risotto perfectly to seafood and light flavours as it won't overwhelm the dish. I like using pipis, clams, lobster and white fish.

arborio This is your everyday risotto workhorse — with arborio you're not making a statement, you're making a meal. I call arborio the user-friendly risotto rice as it can be used with all sorts of ingredients to achieve a suitable result. It can withstand heavy or light flavours. I usually pair arborio with a vegetable and use a stock made from the same vegetable to cook with.

cooking methods

There are three traditional styles of risotto: baked, fried and wet. A baked risotto is where the rice is cooked on the stove with a stock (typically seven parts liquid to one part rice), then finished off in the oven. This creates a timbale or pilaf, which is usually cut and served in slices.

To make a wet risotto, sauté your meat or vegetables in wine and stock, then add the rice and liquid (a little at a time): five parts liquid to one part rice is a good rule of thumb.

For a fried risotto, the rice is cooked like a pilaf in the oven until light and fluffy, then fried in the same manner as Asian fried rice.

risotto con punta di petto brasato
risotto with braised veal skirt

serves 6

Heat the olive oil in a large heavy-based ovenproof saucepan over medium–high heat. Cook the veal until browned all over. Add the carrot, celery and garlic and stir until well coloured.

Add the pancetta and cook for 1–2 minutes or until fragrant. Add the wine and deglaze the pan, scraping the base with a wooden spoon to remove any cooked-on pieces. Simmer until the wine is nearly evaporated. Add the tomato and stock, reduce the heat to as low as possible, cover and simmer for 3 hours or until the veal is meltingly tender. Remove the veal skirt from the pan and, using 2 forks, shred the meat. Return the meat to the pan.

Preheat the oven to 150°C (300°F/Gas 2). Add the rice to the pan, stir well, cover again and bake for 25 minutes or until the rice is al dente. Remove from the oven, stir in the extra virgin olive oil, season to taste with sea salt and freshly ground black pepper and spoon onto flat serving plates.

60 ml (2 fl oz/¼ cup) olive oil
400 g (14 oz) piece of veal skirt
1 small carrot, finely chopped
1 small stalk celery, finely chopped
3 garlic cloves, sliced
150 g (5½ oz) pancetta, cut into 1 cm (½ inch) pieces
250 ml (9 fl oz/1 cup) red wine
800 g (1 lb 12 oz) tinned chopped tomatoes
1 litre (35 fl oz/4 cups) veal stock (see page 264)
300 g (10½ oz) vialone nano rice (see page 140)
1½ tablespoons extra virgin olive oil

This is a wet-style risotto. Here I've infused cream with cauliflower to cook the rice. Remember to rest it for a few minutes and serve it runny on a flat plate (not a bowl) to allow the flavours to infuse properly.

risotto all'ortolano
risotto with cauliflower & fried zucchini serves 6

500 ml (17 fl oz/2 cups) pouring
   (single) cream
1 small head cauliflower
   (about 500 g/1 lb 2 oz), diced
   including stalks
80 ml (2½ fl oz/⅓ cup) olive oil
2 green zucchini (courgettes),
   thinly sliced
2 yellow zucchini (courgettes),
   thinly sliced
750 ml (26 fl oz/3 cups) vegetable
   stock (see page 265)
1 onion, finely chopped
300 g (10½ oz) arborio rice
   (see page 140)
125 ml (4 fl oz/½ cup) white wine
60 g (2¼ oz) butter, chopped
finely grated parmesan, chopped
   flat-leaf (Italian) parsley and
   extra virgin olive oil, to serve

Place the cream and cauliflower in a saucepan over medium heat. Bring to a simmer, then reduce the heat to low, cover and simmer for 30 minutes or until tender. Season to taste with sea salt and freshly ground black pepper. Strain the cauliflower in a sieve placed over a bowl and reserve the cream.

Place the cauliflower and a little of the reserved cream in a blender and purée until smooth. Set aside.

Heat 60 ml (2 fl oz/¼ cup) of the olive oil in a large frying pan over high heat. Cook the zucchini, in batches, until golden on both sides. Drain on absorbent paper, season to taste and set aside.

Place the stock in a saucepan and bring to the boil, then reduce to a simmer.

Heat the remaining olive oil in a heavy-based frying pan over medium heat. Add the onion and cook for 5 minutes or until translucent. Add the rice and stir until coated in oil and heated through. Add the wine and simmer until nearly evaporated. Gradually add the hot stock, 125 ml (4 fl oz/½ cup) at a time, while stirring continuously, until all absorbed. Add the remaining reserved cream, 80 ml (2½ fl oz/ ⅓ cup) at a time, while stirring continuously or until the rice is al dente. Stir in the cauliflower purée and butter and season to taste. Bring to a simmer, then remove from the heat and rest for 5 minutes.

Spoon onto flat serving plates, top with the zucchini, a little of the parmesan and parsley and a drizzle of the extra virgin olive oil to serve.

risotto della riva
flathead & mussel risotto

serves 6

Place the stock in a saucepan over medium heat. Bring to a simmer, then reduce the heat to low and keep at a bare simmer.

Heat half of the oil in a large heavy-based frying pan over medium heat. Add the onion and cook for 4–5 minutes or until softened but not browned. Add the rice and stir until all the grains are coated in oil and heated through. Add the wine and simmer for 1 minute or until nearly evaporated.

Add 125 ml (4 fl oz/½ cup) of the stock and stir until absorbed. Add the remaining stock, 125 ml at a time, allowing each addition to be absorbed before adding the next, while stirring continuously for 15–20 minutes or until the rice is al dente. You need to reserve 125 ml stock for cooking the fish and mussels.

Heat the remaining oil in a separate large heavy-based frying pan over medium–high heat. Cook the fish until browned on both sides, then remove from the pan. Add the tomato, basil and reserved stock to the pan. Bring to a simmer, return the fish to the pan and add the mussels. Cover and cook until the fish starts to flake and the mussels open.

Add to the risotto, then remove from the heat. Gently stir in the butter and season to taste with sea salt and freshly ground black pepper. Allow the risotto to rest for 3 minutes before serving, remembering that the risotto is best served a little runny.

1 litre (35 fl oz/4 cups) fish stock
   (see page 265)
2 tablespoons olive oil
1 onion, finely chopped
300 g (10½ oz) vialone nano rice
   (see page 140)
80 ml (2½ fl oz/⅓ cup) white wine
2 large flathead fillets
   (about 150 g/5½ oz each)
1 punnet cherry tomatoes, halved
12 basil leaves
500 g (1 lb 2 oz) mussels,
   scrubbed and beards removed
125 g (4½ oz) butter, chopped

Risotto should never be dry and dense. It should resemble a flow of molten lava from a volcano. If it is too thick, just stir in some hot stock to loosen it a little.

risotto con taleggio e funghi
taleggio & mushroom risotto

serves 6

1.5 litres (52 fl oz) vegetable stock
  (see page 265)
200 g (7 oz) Taleggio, chopped
120 g (4¼ oz) butter, chopped
1 onion, finely chopped
300 g (10½ oz) arborio rice
  (see page 140)
60 ml (2 fl oz/¼ cup) olive oil
160 g (5¾ oz) frozen porcini (cep)
  mushrooms (see Note),
  defrosted and sliced
150 g (5½ oz) field mushrooms,
  sliced
extra virgin olive oil, for drizzling

Place the stock in a saucepan over medium heat and bring to a simmer. Reduce the heat to low and keep at a bare simmer.

Meanwhile, place the Taleggio in a small saucepan over very low heat and stir for about 10 minutes or until melted. Remove from the heat and keep warm.

Heat the butter in a heavy-based frying pan over low heat. Add the onion and cook for 6–8 minutes or until translucent. Add the rice and stir until the grains are well coated in butter and heated through.

Add 125 ml (4 fl oz/½ cup) of the stock and stir until absorbed. Add the remaining stock, 125 ml at a time, allowing each addition to be absorbed before adding the next, while stirring continuously for about 15–20 minutes or until the rice is al dente.

Stir in the melted Taleggio, season to taste with sea salt and freshly ground black pepper and bring to a gentle simmer. Remove from the heat and allow to rest for about 5 minutes.

While the risotto is resting, heat the olive oil in a large frying pan over high heat. When it just begins to smoke, immediately add the mushrooms. Season to taste and cook, tossing, until golden and tender and the liquid has evaporated. Scatter over the risotto and drizzle with the extra virgin olive oil to serve.

Note Frozen porcini mushrooms are available from good Italian delis and grocers. When in season, you can use fresh porcini.

pasta
a meal for all occasions

Pasta is something that's very close to my heart.
It's my favourite food and a dish I eat every single day.
Some days my wife Justine might not want to eat it, so I
sneak to Mum's place for a bowl. My father is 83 years old
and still eats pasta every day. For him, the day is not right
when he doesn't.

Pasta is a way of life for Italians. As you take the twists
and turns of travel around Italy, each region — often even
each town — has their own pasta shape or sauce, made
with regional or local ingredients, not found anywhere else
in the country. There's Bolognese sauce, of course, from
Bologna, Napoletana sauce from Naples, and dumplings
from Trieste, to name a few.

the science behind pasta

Choosing to use fresh or dried pasta will depend on what sauce you want to serve with it. Homemade pasta sucks in much more flavour than dried pasta but is a very fragile addition to any dish. Fresh is best for broths, thin sauces and light dishes, otherwise the pasta may break to bits in the dish. Don't be afraid to cook fresh pasta more than al dente, if you think it should be softer — it should taste good for you.

Every Italian household always has packets of dried pasta in the pantry. It's a staple in our diet and great to have on hand when you don't have time to make your own. Store-bought pasta holds its shape in rugged, meatier dishes, such as ragù. There are so many shapes available, all of which are fun to experiment with. Never refresh pasta in iced water; it will only turn pale white and gluggy and lose its flavour as the pasta absorbs the water.

When shopping for dried pasta, look for small, reputable makers and choose pasta made with quality durum wheat with no preservatives or unnecessary additives. Australia produces some of the best flours and often these are exported to Italy to make pasta in traditional machines. Always check the 'used by' date as well as the 'made on' date — you want something that has been made within the past 12 months.

perfect pasta every time

In Italy you'll find that pasta is typically made with strong (00) flour which is high in gluten and milled extra fine. What Italians call plain flour is very coarse, more like what we in Australia would call 'wholemeal'. Traditionalists prefer to use strong flour but I find the plain flour in Australia is milled to such a high quality and has a similar level of gluten that it is just as good as strong flour and produces excellent pasta. It's what I use everyday at home and in the restaurant. When making fresh pasta (see page 170), follow these tips and tricks for pasta like a pro.

How to knead Use the fleshy part of one palm to push down on the dough in a gliding motion. At the same time, use your other hand to turn the dough back on itself.

Dough likes a good nap Resting after kneading allows the gluten to relax and the dough will be less lumpy. Shape the dough into a ball, cover and leave.

Pasta sheets fit for sleeping in Roll out
the dough on the widest setting 2–3 times,
then once for each setting thereafter.
Don't forget to dust the rollers with flour.

On a roll When cutting pasta by hand,
roll up your sheets with plenty of flour
sprinkled in between — this makes them
easier to cut and unravel later.

Skinny spaghetti or papa pappardelle?
First, trim the ends of each pasta roll,
so you have neat, straight edges, then
cut each roll to your desired width.

Give it a toss To separate the pasta
strands, gently shake them through
your fingers. They should unravel easily.
Spread over a tray and chill until cooking.

a shape for every sauce

First imagine the sauce you want to cook, then choose a shape to complement it. Orecchiette are like little shovels for small pieces of meat or peas, rotelle are wagon wheels that trap loads of flavour, fusilli are spirals that work perfectly with minced meat and farfalle have an explosion of flavour in the mouth. There is reason to all the different shapes. Below are some examples:

short & hollow Macaroni and other short pastas, such as dried rigatoni and penne, suit light- to medium-bodied sauces. Macaroni is best fresh rather than dried. The dough is rolled onto a stick to shape the pasta, then removed and boiled for about 30 minutes. It's luscious and melts in your mouth but doesn't fall apart.

long & flat Linguine, tagliatelle and pappardelle are mostly bought dried and used in medium- to heavy-bodied, slurpy sauces, such as ragùs made with pork, bacon or beef. The meat clings to each strand as you twirl it around your fork.

long & thin Bucatini, spaghetti and angel hair pastas work well with a finer minced meat sauce, Bolognese, for example. A traditional accompaniment to bucatini is a pork belly, chilli and red sauce called 'amatriciana'. This punchy sauce works its way inside the pasta as well as all around it. Angel hair can't handle heavy sauces; it needs something light that's cooked quickly, such as butter or oil, but never cream.

pasta sheets I prefer to use fresh lasagne and cannelloni pasta sheets as they're lighter on the palate than dried versions and won't weigh the whole dish down. There are, however, good-quality dried lasagne sheets available that don't need to be pre-boiled, just layered with fresh ingredients, then baked.

gnocchi These should be made fresh. I have never had a light and fluffy gnocchi that's been pre-cooked. You can't add too many flavours to gnocchi. Keep it simple and use just one key ingredient: Napoletana sauce, Gorgonzola or fish stock, say.

start to finish

Always use lightly salted, rapidly boiling water to cook pasta in, otherwise it loses its flavour. To finish, drizzle over extra virgin olive oil instead of cooking with it as it will burn in the pan and lose its flavour. And remember pasta is never about quantity, but always quality.

bucatini con pancetta di maiale
bucatini with pork belly

serves 6

Preheat the oven to 140°C (275°F/Gas 1).

Place the pork belly in a roasting tray, skin-side up. Brush with the extra oil, then scatter over the rosemary and sage and a little sea salt and bake for 4 hours or until the meat begins to fall apart.

Remove from the oven, cool and refrigerate for 2 hours.

Heat the oil in a heavy-based saucepan over medium heat. Add the onion and garlic and cook for 5 minutes or until translucent. Add the tomato and bring to the boil, then reduce the heat to low and simmer, stirring regularly, for 45 minutes. Add the basil and peas and simmer for another 15 minutes.

Remove the pork belly from the fridge. Remove the skin and discard. Cut the meat into 1 cm (½ inch) cubes, add to the sauce and simmer for another 10 minutes. Season to taste with sea salt and black pepper.

Just before serving, cook the bucatini in a large saucepan of lightly salted boiling water. Stir gently to stop the pasta from sticking together. Cook until al dente, then drain. Add the pasta to the sauce, then stir in the butter. Serve with plenty of parmesan.

500 g (1 lb 2 oz) boneless pork belly, skin on
2 tablespoons olive oil, plus extra for brushing
1 teaspoon rosemary leaves
5 sage leaves
1 white onion, sliced
6 garlic cloves, sliced
800 g (1 lb 12 oz) tinned chopped tomatoes
12 basil leaves
150 g (5½ oz) fresh or frozen peas
500 g (1 lb 2 oz) dried bucatini
60 g (2¼ oz) butter, chopped
finely grated parmesan, to serve

When you need more than one serviette for chunky, slurpy pastas, like this one, it means it is good!

malfatti con stinco di agnello e piselli
malfatti with lamb shanks & peas

serves 6

4 lamb shanks

60 ml (2 fl oz/¼ cup) olive oil

1 star anise

3 cloves

1 onion, finely chopped

1 small leek, white part only, finely chopped

1 small carrot, finely chopped

1 small stalk celery, finely chopped

1 bay leaf

1 litre (35 fl oz/4 cups) chicken stock (see page 264)

250 g (9 oz) fresh or frozen peas

1 small handful flat-leaf (Italian) parsley leaves, chopped

500 g (1 lb 2 oz) dried malfatti

1½ tablespoons extra virgin olive oil

finely grated parmesan, to serve

Season the shanks to taste with sea salt and freshly ground black pepper. Heat the olive oil in a large heavy-based saucepan over medium–high heat. Cook the shanks until browned all over, then remove from the pan. Add the spices, onion, leek, carrot, celery and bay leaf and cook, stirring occasionally, for 5 minutes or until the vegetables begin to caramelise.

Return the shanks to the pan, add the stock, reduce the heat to low, then cover and simmer gently for 2 hours or until the meat begins to fall off the bones.

Remove the shanks from the pan and set aside. Increase the heat to high and simmer the sauce until reduced by two-thirds.

Return the shanks to the pan, add the peas and parsley and season to taste. Simmer for another 30 minutes or until the sauce has thickened. Remove the shanks from the pan and shred the meat from the bones. Return the meat to the sauce.

Meanwhile, cook the malfatti in a large saucepan of salted boiling water until al dente. Drain, then return to the pan. Add the sauce and the extra virgin olive oil. Toss to combine well, season to taste and serve with plenty of parmesan.

pennette con polpo brasato
pennette with braised octopus

serves 6

Preheat the oven to 140°C (275°F/Gas 1).

Heat 60 ml (2 fl oz/¼ cup) of the olive oil in a large ovenproof saucepan over medium heat. Add the onion and garlic and cook for 5 minutes or until translucent. Add the octopus and tomato, toss to combine well and bake for 25 minutes or until the octopus is tender.

Meanwhile, pound the anchovies, capers and herbs in a mortar with a pestle until a smooth paste forms.

When the octopus is tender, remove from the oven and place over low heat. Stir in the anchovy mixture and simmer for 10 minutes or until the octopus is very tender.

Meanwhile, cook the pennette in a large saucepan of lightly salted boiling water until al dente. Drain, then add to the octopus mixture, season to taste with sea salt and freshly ground black pepper and toss to combine well. Stand for 2–3 minutes before serving to allow the sauce to be absorbed by the pasta. Drizzle with the extra virgin olive oil to serve.

80 ml (2½ fl oz/⅓ cup) olive oil
1 onion, thinly sliced
4 garlic cloves, sliced
1.2 kg (2 lb 10 oz) baby octopus, cleaned and halved
2 punnets cherry tomatoes, halved
10 white anchovy fillets
15 salted baby capers, rinsed
12 basil leaves
¼ cup flat-leaf (Italian) parsley leaves
500 g (1 lb 2 oz) dried pennette
extra virgin olive oil, for drizzling

linguine all'aglio e olio con gamberi

linguine with garlic, oil & prawns

serves 4

375 g (13 oz) dried linguine

80 ml (2½ fl oz/⅓ cup) extra
   virgin olive oil, plus extra
   for drizzling

4 garlic cloves, sliced

4 anchovy fillets, chopped

1 tablespoon confit red chilli
   (see page 263) or 1 long red
   chilli, seeds removed and
   thinly sliced

20 raw medium prawns (shrimp),
   peeled and deveined and
   halved lengthways

1 medium handful flat-leaf (Italian)
   parsley leaves, chopped

poor man's parmesan
   (see page 263), to serve

Cook the linguine in a large saucepan of salted boiling water until al dente, then drain.

Meanwhile, heat the oil in a large heavy-based frying pan over high heat. Add the garlic and cook until it just starts to brown and crisp up. Add the anchovy and chilli and stir for 1 minute. Add the prawns and parsley, season to taste with sea salt and freshly ground black pepper — keeping in mind that the anchovies are salty — then toss for 1–2 minutes or until the prawns are just cooked through.

Add the linguine to the prawn mixture, reduce the heat to low and toss until the linguini is well coated. Serve immediately, drizzled with a little of the oil and scattered with the poor man's parmesan.

orecchiette con broccolini e pecorino fresco
orecchiette with broccolini & pecorino

serves 6–8

Cook the orecchietti in a large saucepan of salted boiling water until al dente. Drain and reserve 125 ml (4 fl oz/½ cup) of the cooking water.

Meanwhile, heat the oil in a large frying pan over medium–high heat. Add the onion and celery and cook for 5 minutes or until caramelised. Add the broccolini and mushrooms, season to taste with sea salt and freshly ground black pepper and stir until the mushrooms and broccolini begin to colour and caramelise.

Add the pine nuts and parsley and combine well. Stir in the reserved cooking water, then add the butter and combine well.

Add the orecchiette, season to taste and toss to combine. Serve scattered with the pecorino.

500 g (1 lb 2 oz) dried orecchiette
60 ml (2 fl oz/¼ cup) extra virgin olive oil
1 small onion, finely chopped
1 small stalk celery, finely chopped
3 bunches broccolini, chopped
5 field mushrooms, sliced
50 g (1¾ oz/⅓ cup) pine nuts, toasted
1 medium handful flat-leaf (Italian) parsley leaves
100 g (3½ oz) butter, chopped
shaved pecorino, to serve

spaghetti al nero di sepia
spaghetti with squid ink & cuttlefish

serves 6

Heat the oil in a large frying pan over low heat. Add the anchovies and parsley and stir for 2 minutes or until the anchovies are dissolved. Add the cuttlefish, then the Napoletana sauce and bring to a simmer. Stir in the squid ink paste and simmer for 30–35 minutes or until the cuttlefish is tender. Remove from the heat and season to taste with sea salt and freshly ground black pepper.

Meanwhile, cook the spaghetti in a large saucepan of salted boiling water until al dente. Drain, add to the sauce, then toss until the spaghetti is well coated. Stand for 2–3 minutes before serving to allow the sauce to be absorbed by the pasta.

Note Squid ink paste is available from good delis and fishmongers.

60 ml (2 fl oz/¼ cup) olive oil
5 anchovy fillets
1 small handful flat-leaf (Italian) parsley leaves, chopped
400 g (14 oz) cuttlefish, cleaned and thinly sliced
500 ml (17 fl oz/2 cups) Napoletana sauce (see page 262)
2 tablespoons squid ink paste (see Note)
500 g (1 lb 2 oz) dried spaghetti

Use good-quality already picked crab meat. If you have to pick the crab meat yourself, it will take away the enjoyment of this simple dish.

pappardelle con granchio, basilico e pomodorini
pappardelle with crab, basil & cherry tomatoes

serves 6

2 punnets cherry tomatoes, halved
300 g (10½ oz) cooked picked
    crab meat
12 basil leaves, torn
500 g (1 lb 2 oz) dried pappardelle
60 ml (2 fl oz/¼ cup) extra virgin
    olive oil

Preheat the oven to 140°C (275°F/Gas 1).

Place the tomato halves, cut-side up, on a baking tray and bake for 15 minutes or until they begin to shrivel up. Place in a large bowl, add the crab meat and basil and stir gently to combine.

Cook the pappardelle in a large saucepan of salted boiling water until al dente. Drain and reserve 100 ml (3½ fl oz) of the cooking water.

Add the pappardelle to the crab mixture along with the reserved cooking water. Season to taste with sea salt and freshly ground black pepper and toss until the pappardelle is well coated. There should be enough 'sauce' to coat the pasta. If not, add a little extra reserved cooking water. Drizzle over the oil, toss again to coat and serve.

pasta all'uovo
fresh egg pasta sheets

makes about 500 g (1 lb 2 oz)

400 g (14 oz/2 ⅔ cups) plain
(all-purpose) flour,
plus extra for dusting
4 eggs
2 tablespoons olive oil

Place the flour in a large bowl and make a well in the centre. Crack the eggs into the well, then add the oil and a pinch of sea salt and whisk with a fork to combine. Start adding the flour to the wet ingredients by bringing it in a little at a time from the well until the mixture comes together. Turn out and knead until a dough forms, adding a little extra flour, if the dough feels sticky, or a little water if it feels dry. Knead until the dough is smooth and satiny. (Alternatively, you can place the dough in the bowl of an electric mixer with a dough hook attachment and knead for 5 minutes or until smooth and satiny.) Wrap in plastic wrap and refrigerate for 1 hour.

Divide the dough into 4 pieces. Working with 1 piece at a time, and keeping the others covered to prevent them drying out, lightly dust the first piece of dough with flour and roll through a pasta machine on the widest setting 2–3 times, then once for each setting thereafter until the pasta is 1–1.5 mm (1/16 inch) thick. Place on a lightly floured tray, cover with a slightly damp tea towel and repeat with the remaining dough. Use as directed in recipes.

rotolo di ricotta e spinaci
ricotta & spinach roll

serves 8

Place the ricotta, spinach, parmesan, parsley and egg in a bowl and combine well. Season to taste with sea salt and freshly ground black pepper and combine again. Set aside.

Lightly dampen a work surface and place a 40 cm (16 inch) long piece of plastic wrap on top, with the long side facing you (the dampness stops the plastic from slipping).

Cook 2 pasta sheets in a large saucepan of lightly salted boiling water for 1 minute. Remove with a large slotted spoon and drain well. While the pasta sheets are still hot, place on top of the plastic with one long side slightly overlapping. Spread half of the filling all over the pasta sheets, leaving a 3 cm (1¼ inch) border along the top and a 2 cm (¾ inch) border along the bottom.

Starting from the bottom and, using the plastic wrap as a guide, roll the pasta sheets over, separating the plastic wrap from the pasta as you go. The end result should be a log, with a cross-section resembling a snail shell with layers of pasta and spinach. Place on a large tray and freeze for 1 hour to firm up. Repeat with the remaining pasta sheets and filling.

Preheat the oven to 170°C (325°F/Gas 3).

Remove the chilled rotolo from the freezer, unwrap and cut into 2 cm (¾ inch) thick slices.

Cover the bases of 2 large baking dishes each with one-third of the Napoletana sauce. Arrange the rotolo slices on top in a single layer. Top each slice with the remaining sauce, scatter over the extra grated parmesan and bake for 20 minutes or until hot and bubbling. Drizzle with the oil and scatter over extra parmesan to serve.

400 g (14 oz) fresh ricotta
200 g (7 oz) baby spinach leaves, blanched and squeezed dry, then coarsely chopped
150 g (5½ oz) finely grated parmesan, plus extra for sprinkling
½ cup coarsely chopped flat-leaf (Italian) parsley leaves
2 eggs, lightly beaten
1 quantity fresh egg pasta sheets (4 in total) (see opposite)
750 ml (26 fl oz/3 cups) Napoletana sauce (see page 262)
extra virgin olive oil, for drizzling

fettuccine alla carbonara
fettuccine carbonara

serves 6

Working with one pasta sheet at a time, dust the first sheet generously with flour all over. Roll up and, using a large sharp knife, cut it into 8 mm (⅜ inch) wide strips. Alternatively, fit your pasta machine with the fettuccine-cutting attachment and feed the sheets through, one at a time.

To separate the strands, gently shake the fettuccine through your fingers and spread over a large tray and refrigerate, uncovered, for 30 minutes. This makes the pasta easier to work with.

Place the egg yolks and parmesan in a small bowl. Season to taste with sea salt and freshly ground black pepper and lightly beat with a fork. Set aside.

Place the pancetta in a large non-stick frying pan over medium heat and cook until crisp, then remove the pan from the heat.

Just before the pancetta is ready, cook the fettuccine in a large saucepan of salted boiling water for 2 minutes or until the pasta floats to the top. Drain, reserving 2 tablespoons of the cooking water.

Add the fettuccine to the frying pan, toss to coat, then add the reserved cooking water. Stir in the egg yolk mixture and toss to combine well. Serve immediately, sprinkled with extra parmesan.

1 quantity fresh egg pasta sheets
    (see page 170)
plain (all-purpose) flour,
    for dusting
6 egg yolks
100 g (3½ oz/1 cup) finely grated
    parmesan, plus extra to serve
150 g (5½ oz) pancetta,
    thinly sliced

spaghetti alle vongole
spaghetti with clams

serves 6

1 quantity fresh egg pasta sheets
    (see page 170)
plain (all-purpose) flour,
    for dusting
125 ml (4 fl oz/½ cup) olive oil
6 garlic cloves, sliced
1 medium handful flat-leaf (Italian)
    parsley leaves, chopped
1 kg (2 lb 4 oz) clams (vongole),
    soaked for 2 hours in several
    changes of cold water
125 ml (4 fl oz/½ cup) white wine
2 ox heart tomatoes, peeled
    and finely chopped
extra virgin olive oil, for drizzling
poor man's parmesan
    (see page 263), to serve

Working with one pasta sheet at a time, dust the first sheet generously with flour all over. Roll up and, using a large sharp knife, cut it into 2 mm (1/16 inch) wide strips. Alternatively, fit your pasta machine with the spaghetti-cutting attachment and feed the sheets through, one at a time.

To separate the strands, gently shake the spaghetti through your fingers and spread over a large tray and refrigerate, uncovered, for 30 minutes. This makes the pasta easier to work with.

Cook the spaghetti in a large saucepan of lightly salted boiling water for 2–3 minutes or until the pasta floats to the top, then drain.

Meanwhile, heat the olive oil in a large deep frying pan over high heat. Add the garlic and cook for 2 minutes or until just golden. Add the parsley and clams and stir to coat. Add the wine, cover and simmer until the clams open. Add the tomato, stir to combine, then add the spaghetti and toss until well combined. Season to taste with sea salt and freshly ground black pepper. Divide among bowls, drizzle with the extra virgin olive oil and scatter over the poor man's parmesan to serve.

pappardelle con salsiccia
pappardelle with sausage

serves 6

Working with one pasta sheet at a time, dust the first sheet generously with flour all over. Roll up and, using a large sharp knife, cut it into 1.5 cm (⅝ inch) wide strips.

To separate the strands, gently shake the pasta through your fingers and spread over a large tray and refrigerate, uncovered, for 30 minutes. This makes the pasta easier to work with.

Heat the oil in a large frying pan over medium–high heat. Crumble the sausage meat into the pan and cook, breaking the meat up into small pieces, until browned all over.

Meanwhile, cook the pappardelle in a large saucepan of lightly salted boiling water for 2 minutes or until the pasta floats to the top. Drain, then return to the pan and place over low heat.

Add the cooked sausage, including any oil, to the pappardelle and toss to combine well. Gradually add the butter and parmesan, season to taste with sea salt and freshly ground black pepper and gently toss to coat well. Serve with the extra parmesan scattered over.

1 quantity fresh egg pasta sheets (see page 170)
plain (all-purpose) flour, for dusting
80 ml (2½ fl oz/⅓ cup) olive oil
300 g (10½ oz) Italian sausages, casings removed
60 g (2¼ oz) butter, chopped and softened
35 g (1¼ oz/⅓ cup) finely grated parmesan, plus extra to serve

ravioli di gamberi
prawn ravioli

serves 6

300 g (10½ oz) peeled raw
    prawns (shrimp), deveined
2 egg whites
1 tablespoon chopped flat-leaf
    (Italian) parsley, plus
    extra whole leaves
zest of ¼ lemon
1 quantity fresh egg pasta sheets
    (see page 170)
plain (all-purpose) flour,
    for dusting
5 cherry tomatoes, thinly sliced
100 g (3½ oz) fresh ricotta
2 tablespoons milk, warmed
extra virgin olive oil, for drizzling

Chop two-thirds of the prawns and set aside. Place the remaining prawns in a blender. Add 1 egg white and season to taste with sea salt and freshly ground black pepper, then process until a smooth mousse forms. Transfer to a bowl, add the chopped prawns, chopped parsley and lemon zest, combine well and season to taste.

Working with one pasta sheet at a time, lay the first sheet on a lightly floured work surface. Beginning 2 cm (¾ inch) from the corner of the sheet, place tablespoons of prawn mixture, 2 cm (¾ inch) apart, along the centre of the sheet. Place some tomato and a parsley leaf on top of each mound.

Lightly beat the remaining egg white and use it to lightly brush the edges of the pasta sheet. Take another pasta sheet and place it on top, pressing it down around the prawn filling, ensuring there are no air pockets, then using a 4 cm (1½ inch) round pastry cutter, lightly press down around each filling to make an indent making sure not to cut through the pasta. Using a 5 cm (2 inch) round pastry cutter, cut out each round and place, without touching, on a large tea towel lined tray. Refrigerate, uncovered, for 30 minutes.

Meanwhile, place the ricotta and warm milk in a large bowl. Season to taste and combine well. Transfer to a large serving dish.

Cook the ravioli, in batches, in a large saucepan of lightly salted boiling water. When they float to the top, cook for 1 minute more, then remove using a slotted spoon. Drain, then place on top of the ricotta sauce and drizzle with extra virgin olive oil.

The trick to making lighter-than-air gnocchi is to use old potatoes — ones that have started to sprout which means the starches have started to break down. Also, baking the potatoes on a bed of rock salt draws out the moisture and makes for a fluffier result.

gnocchi

serves 6

1 kg (2 lb 4 oz) large, old desiree
    potatoes, unpeeled and washed
500 g (1 lb 2 oz) rock salt
100 g (3½ oz) butter, softened
    and chopped
150 g (5½ oz/1½ cups) finely
    grated parmesan
3 egg yolks
150 g (5½ oz/1 cup) plain
    (all-purpose) flour,
    plus extra, for dusting

Preheat the oven to 190°C (375°F/Gas 5).

Place the potatoes in a large saucepan of cold water, bring to a simmer and cook until tender. The trick is to cook the potatoes slowly, keeping the skins intact. Using a slotted spoon, remove the potatoes from the water, being careful not to break the skins. Spread the rock salt over a baking tray, then place the hot potatoes on top and bake for 20 minutes or until the skins begin to blister.

For the next step, it's important to work quickly as the mixture must remain hot. Working with one potato at a time, halve the potato. Hold one half in a tea towel and scoop out the flesh. Press the hot flesh through a potato ricer into a bowl. Add the butter, parmesan, egg yolks, flour and 1 teaspoon sea salt in that order. Mix together thoroughly, then turn the dough out onto a lightly floured surface.

Divide the dough into 10 pieces. Roll each portion into a 2 cm (¾ inch) thick log. Using a small knife, cut each log into 2 cm (¾ inch) lengths. (At this stage you can fill the fresh gnocchi, see page 182.)

You can leave the gnocchi as they are or gently roll with a gnocchi paddle or fork to create grooves which catch the sauce. I prefer to freeze the gnocchi before cooking to make them less fragile. Place the gnocchi on a tray, without touching, and freeze for 15 minutes. If you're not cooking immediately, transfer the frozen gnocchi to a zip-lock bag and store in the freezer for up to 5 weeks. Cook frozen gnocchi, without defrosting, as directed in recipes.

gnocchi al taleggio
taleggio-filled gnocchi

serves 6

1 quantity fresh (not yet frozen)
    gnocchi (see page 180)
plain (all-purpose) flour,
    for dusting
200 g (7 oz) Taleggio, cut into
    1 cm (½ inch) cubes
1 egg, lightly beaten
60 ml (2 fl oz/¼ cup) olive oil
180 g (6½ oz) frozen porcini (cep)
    mushrooms (see Note),
    defrosted, patted dry and
    thinly sliced
3 garlic cloves, sliced
500 ml (17 fl oz/2 cups) chicken
    stock (see page 264)
extra virgin olive oil, for drizzling
100 g (3½ oz/1 cup) finely grated
    pecorino

Place a single gnocchi on a well-floured work surface and, using a rolling pin, gently flatten out into a 3 mm (⅛ inch) thick circle.

Place a piece of Taleggio in the centre of the gnocchi and lightly brush the edges with beaten egg. Using well-floured fingers, pick up the gnocchi and fold into a half-moon shape, pressing the edge to seal. Place on a lightly floured tray and repeat with the remaining gnocchi and Taleggio. Make sure the gnocchi do not touch.

Heat the olive oil in a frying pan over high heat. Add the porcini, season to taste with sea salt and freshly ground black pepper and cook until golden and crisp. Add the garlic and once it starts to brown, remove the pan from the heat. Set aside and keep warm.

Place the stock in a large saucepan and bring to a simmer. Season to taste. Cook the gnocchi, in batches, until they float to the surface. You just want to poach the gnocchi gently. Remove with a slotted spoon.

To serve, spread the porcini mushrooms over the base of each bowl, place the gnocchi on top and pour over just enough stock to cover the mushrooms. Drizzle with the extra virgin olive oil and sprinkle over the pecorino.

Note Frozen porcini mushrooms are available from Italian delis and grocers. You can also use fresh, when in season.

gnocchi alla napoletana
gnocchi napoletana

serves 6

Place the Napoletana sauce in a large frying pan over medium heat and cook until hot.

Meanwhile, cook the frozen gnocchi, in batches, in a large saucepan of lightly salted boiling water. As soon as they float to the surface they are cooked. Remove with a slotted spoon and place in the hot sauce. Gently shake the pan to coat the gnocchi, but do not toss or stir or they will break apart.

Pour out onto a flat plate, drizzle with the oil and sprinkle over the parmesan to serve.

750 ml (26 fl oz/3 cups) Napoletana sauce (see page 262)
1 quantity frozen gnocchi (see page 180)
extra virgin olive oil, for drizzling
100 g (3½ oz/1 cup) finely grated parmesan

piatti unici
one-pan wonders

What could be easier than one pan to cook in, one pan to eat from and one pan to clean. These dishes are deceptively simple, but rely on good ingredients and a cook who knows what they're doing. About 60 per cent of my restaurant menu features these kinds of dishes because they are so simple to make yet pack a punch in flavour.

Whenever I hire a new chef, I always ask him to cook me some kind of piatti unici. If they can pull off a tasty dish, it means they understand cooking times, heat and seasoning — all essentials in the kitchen. I hope the recipes in this chapter will help you on your way to understanding the art of piatti unici.

mix 'n' match

It doesn't matter what you use to cook the recipes in this chapter: one pan, one pot or one casserole dish, it's just about the concentration of flavours. The beauty of these dishes is that they're layered, seasoned and finished in the same moment… Just bring the pan to the table and serve straight out of it, so there's no need to plate up.

Make the most of the simplicity of this style of cooking and finish your dish with whatever you love. Throw in some mushrooms, buffalo mozzarella, figs, celery leaves or herbs and enjoy. It's about how you're feeling in the moment, just remember to respect your ingredients and let them shine in your cooking. Here are a couple of my favourites which are so simple and quick that there's no need for a recipe.

braciole
Growing up, this was one of my favourites. It's thinned-out pieces of veal which are filled and rolled up. You can fill them with anything you have in your fridge: olives, Bolognese sauce, meatballs, stuffing… Brown off the rolls in a pan, add some Napoletana sauce, then pop the pan in a moderate oven for 10 minutes to finish cooking.

acqua pazza
I adore snapper and pipis cooked in a pan with a bit of 'acqua pazza', which means 'crazy water'. It's traditionally seawater but I use sparkling mineral water. When the water comes to the boil, I remove the seafood, add a bit of fregola, let it steam off the heat and five minutes later I have the most beautiful simple dish.

pollo alla parmigiana
chicken parmigiana

serves 6

Preheat the oven to 220°C (425°F/Gas 7).

Cut the eggplant lengthways, into six 1 cm (½ inch) thick slices.

Heat 1 cm (½ inch) of oil in a large ovenproof frying pan over high heat. Cook the eggplant, in batches, until golden on both sides, adding more oil to the pan, as necessary. Drain on absorbent paper and set aside.

Return the pan to the heat. Dust the chicken in the seasoned flour, shaking off any excess. Add a little more oil to the pan, if necessary, and cook the chicken, in batches, until browned on both sides. Remove from the pan and place on a plate.

Wipe the excess oil from the pan and place over medium heat. Add the Napoletana sauce and bring to a simmer. Return the chicken to the pan, stir through the butter and simmer for 6–7 minutes or until the chicken is cooked through and the sauce is thickened.

Meanwhile, lay the eggplant slices on top of the chicken, then the basil leaves. Top with the mozzarella, then sprinkle with parmesan and bake for 6 minutes or until the mozzarella has melted.

1 large eggplant (aubergine)
olive oil, for shallow-frying
6 skinless chicken thigh fillets
plain (all-purpose) flour, seasoned, for dusting
750 ml (26 fl oz/3 cups) Napoletana sauce (see page 262)
40 g (1½ oz) butter, chopped
6 basil leaves
3 buffalo mozzarella balls, sliced
80 g (2¾ oz) finely grated parmesan

scaloppine al marsala
veal marsala

serves 4

8 thin slices veal scaloppine
    from the leg or loin
    (about 100 g/3½ oz each)
plain (all-purpose) flour,
    seasoned, for dusting
60 ml (2 fl oz/¼ cup) olive oil
60 ml (2 fl oz/¼ cup) Marsala
125 ml (4 fl oz/½ cup) veal
    (see page 264) or beef stock
250 ml (9 fl oz/1 cup) double
    (thick) cream
2 tablespoons finely chopped
    flat-leaf (Italian) parsley leaves

Using the flat side of a meat mallet, gently flatten the veal between plastic wrap until they are 3–4 mm (⅛ inch) thick all over. Dust the scaloppine in the seasoned flour.

Heat half of the oil in a large frying pan over medium–high heat. Cook half of the veal until just golden on both sides, then remove from the pan. Repeat with the remaining oil and veal.

Tip any excess oil from the pan, then place the pan over medium heat. Add the Marsala and simmer until reduced by half. Add the stock and simmer until reduced by half, then add the cream and simmer until reduced by half again. Return the veal to the pan, turn to coat and simmer for 2–3 minutes or until the sauce thickens and the veal is heated through. Season to taste with sea salt and freshly ground black pepper. Stir through the parsley and serve.

costolette d'agnello al vino rosso
lamb chops in red wine

serves 4–6

60 ml (2 fl oz/¼ cup) olive oil
8 French shallots, halved if large
12 lamb loin chops
2 garlic cloves, thinly sliced
2 teaspoons rosemary leaves
60 g (2¼ oz/½ cup) green olives,
   pitted
250 ml (9 fl oz/1 cup) red wine
1 tablespoon red wine vinegar
50 g (1¾ oz) butter, chopped

Heat 1 tablespoon of the oil in a large heavy-based saucepan over high heat. Cook the shallots for 6–8 minutes or until golden, then remove from the pan and set aside.

Add the remaining oil and cook the lamb chops, in batches, until browned on both sides. Add the garlic, rosemary and olives and stir until the fragrance begins to waft up. Add the wine and bring to a simmer. Decrease the heat to low, return the shallots to the pan, cover and simmer for 30 minutes or until the meat is tender. Stir in the vinegar and season to taste with sea salt and freshly ground black pepper. Remove from the heat, stir in the butter and serve.

filetto al pepe verde
beef fillet with green peppercorns

serves 4

Using a mortar and pestle, crush the peppercorns and combine with the sea salt. Place on a plate and coat the steaks on both sides with the spice mixture.

Heat the oil in a large frying pan over high heat. Cook the steaks until browned on both sides. Remove from the pan and set aside.

Add the wine to the pan and simmer until reduced by half. Add the stock and simmer until reduced by half again. Add the vinegar and season to taste with sea salt and freshly ground black pepper.

Return the steaks and any resting juices to the pan and simmer for 2 minutes each side for medium-rare or until the steaks are cooked to your liking. Remove the steaks from the pan and keep warm.

Continue to simmer the sauce until reduced by one-third, then season to taste. Serve the steaks with the green peppercorn sauce poured over.

1 x 50 g (1½ oz) tin green
    peppercorns in brine, drained
1 tablespoon sea salt flakes
4 centre-cut fillet steaks
    (about 160 g/5¾ oz each)
2 tablespoons olive oil
60 ml (2 fl oz/¼ cup) red wine
250 ml (9 fl oz/1 cup) veal
    (see page 264) or beef stock
1½ tablespoons balsamic vinegar

scaloppine alla pizzaiola
veal pizzaiola

serves 4

Using the flat side of a meat mallet, gently flatten the veal between plastic wrap until they are 3–4 mm (⅛ inch) thick all over. Dust the veal in the seasoned flour.

Heat half of the olive oil in a large frying pan over medium–high heat. Cook half of the veal until just golden on both sides, then remove from the pan. Repeat with the remaining oil and veal.

Wipe any excess oil from the pan, then return the pan to the heat. Add the Napoletana sauce, olives and oregano and simmer for 5 minutes.

Return the veal to the pan, turn to coat and simmer for another 1–2 minutes or until just heated through. Season to taste with sea salt and freshly ground black pepper, drizzle with the extra virgin olive oil and serve.

8 thin slices veal scaloppine
  from the leg or loin
  (about 100 g/3½ oz each)
plain (all-purpose) flour,
  seasoned, for dusting
60 ml (2 fl oz/¼ cup) olive oil
500 ml (17 fl oz/2 cups)
  Napoletana sauce
  (see page 262)
60 g (2¼ oz/½ cup) black olives,
  pitted
2 tablespoons oregano leaves
extra virgin olive oil, for drizzling

pollo alla cacciatora
chicken cacciatore

serves 4

2 tablespoons olive oil

4 chicken supremes, skin on

1 small white onion, thinly sliced

2 teaspoons rosemary leaves,
    finely chopped

4 sage leaves

1 bay leaf

3 garlic cloves, thinly sliced

60 ml (2 fl oz/¼ cup) white wine

60 g (2¼ oz/½ cup) black olives,
    pitted

375 ml (13 fl oz/1½ cups)
    Napoletana sauce
    (see page 262)

1 long red chilli, seeds removed
    and chopped, or 1 tablespoon
    confit red chilli (see page 263)

6 small capsicums (peppers),
    roasted until skins blacken,
    peeled and seeds removed,
    and sliced

ciabatta bread, to serve
    (see page 74)

Heat the oil in a large frying pan over high heat. Cook the chicken until browned all over. Remove from the pan and set aside.

Add the onion and herbs to the pan and cook for 3–4 minutes or until the onion is just softened. Add the garlic and cook for another minute. Add the wine and simmer until reduced by half.

Add the olives, Napoletana sauce, chilli and roasted capsicum. Bring to a simmer, then return the chicken to the pan and simmer for another 8–10 minutes, turning once, or until the chicken is cooked through. Serve the chicken with the sauce spooned over and the ciabatta on the side.

filetto al limone
beef fillet with lemon

serves 4

4 centre-cut fillet steaks
    (about 160 g/5¾ oz each)
2 tablespoons olive oil
125 ml (4 fl oz/½ cup) white wine
2 lemons, juiced, then quartered
½ bunch sage, leaves picked
200 g (7 oz) butter, chopped

Season the steaks on both sides with sea salt and freshly ground black pepper. Heat the oil in a large frying pan over medium–high heat. Cook the steaks until browned on both sides. Remove from the pan and set aside.

Tip any excess oil from the pan and place over high heat. Add the wine and simmer until reduced by half. Add the lemon juice, the squeezed lemon quarters and the sage. Simmer until reduced by half and season to taste.

Return the steaks to the pan and simmer for 2 minutes each side for medium-rare or until cooked to your liking. Remove the steaks from the pan and keep warm.

Decrease the heat to low, add the butter to the pan and stir until the sauce thickens. Do not bring to a simmer or the sauce will split. Season to taste. Serve the steaks with the lemon sauce poured over.

scaloppine ai funghi
veal with mushrooms

serves 4

Using the flat side of a meat mallet, gently flatten the veal between plastic wrap until they are 3–4 mm (⅛ inch) thick all over. Dust the veal in the seasoned flour.

Heat 1½ tablespoons of the oil in a large frying pan over medium-high heat. Cook half of the veal until just golden on both sides, then remove from the pan. Repeat with another 1½ tablespoons oil and the remaining veal, then remove from the pan.

Add the remaining oil to the pan and increase the heat to high. Add the mushroom and toss until golden and tender. Add the wine, reduce the heat to medium and simmer until reduced by half. Add the stock and simmer until reduced by half, then add the cream and simmer until reduced by half again.

Return the veal to the pan, turn to coat, and simmer for 2–3 minutes or until the sauce thickens and the veal is heated through. Season to taste with sea salt and freshly ground black pepper. Stir through the parsley and serve.

8 thin slices veal scaloppine
    from the leg or loin
    (about 100 g/3½ oz each)
plain (all-purpose) flour,
    seasoned, for dusting
125 ml (4 fl oz/½ cup) olive oil
3 large field mushrooms,
    thinly sliced
60 ml (2 fl oz/¼ cup) white wine
125 ml (4 fl oz/½ cup) veal
    (see page 264) or beef stock
250 ml (9 fl oz/1 cup) double
    (thick) cream
2 tablespoons coarsely chopped
    flat-leaf (Italian) parsley leaves

dentice all'agro dolce
snapper with sweet & sour celery

serves 4

125 ml (4 fl oz/½ cup) olive oil
6–8 French shallots, thinly sliced
1 stalk celery, finely chopped
2 teaspoons marjoram leaves
1 small cinnamon stick
1 star anise
75 g (2¾ oz) caster (superfine)
    sugar
75 ml (2½ fl oz) red wine vinegar
½ cup celery leaves, from
    the centre stalks only
1 tablespoon extra virgin olive oil
plain (all-purpose) flour,
    seasoned, for dusting
4 plate-sized snapper fillets,
    skin on

Heat 2 tablespoons of the olive oil in a heavy-based saucepan over high heat. Add the shallot and cook for 2 minutes or until translucent. Add the celery, marjoram, cinnamon and star anise and stir for 5 minutes. Stir in the sugar and cook for another 10 minutes or until the sugar starts to caramelise, but the celery still has some bite.

Add the vinegar, simmer until reduced by half, then remove from the heat. Stir in the celery leaves and stand until cooled to room temperature. Stir in the extra virgin olive oil and season to taste with sea salt and freshly ground black pepper.

Dust the snapper fillets in the seasoned flour, shaking off any excess.

Heat another 2 tablespoons of the olive oil in a large non-stick frying pan over high heat. Cook half of the snapper fillets, skin-side down first, until golden. Turn and cook for another 30 seconds, then remove from the pan and repeat with the remaining olive oil and fish. Serve the snapper fillets topped with the sweet and sour celery.

pescespada in umido
swordfish with tomato & olives

serves 4

Heat the olive oil in a large deep frying pan over medium heat. Cook the shallot for 5 minutes or until translucent. Add the olives, caperberries and celery and cook for another 5 minutes or until the celery is translucent. Add the wine and simmer for 3–4 minutes, then add the tomato and parsley. Simmer for 5 minutes or until the sauce starts to come together.

Place the swordfish in the pan in a single layer, reduce the heat to low, cover with a lid and simmer for 8–10 minutes or until just cooked through.

Remove the swordfish from the pan and rest on a plate for 5 minutes. Season the sauce to taste with sea salt and freshly ground black pepper and stir in the extra virgin olive oil. Serve the swordfish with the sauce poured over.

60 ml (2 fl oz/¼ cup) olive oil
3 French shallots, quartered
60 g (2¼ oz/½ cup) pitted
    green olives
10 caperberries
1 small stalk celery, finely chopped
60 ml (2 fl oz/¼ cup) white wine
3 tomatoes, peeled and chopped
1 small handful flat-leaf (Italian)
    parsley leaves
4 swordfish fillets
    (about 180 g/6½ oz each)
1½ tablespoons extra virgin
    olive oil

anatra al forno
slow-baked duck

serves 4

2 ducks (about 1.7 kg/
3 lb 12 oz each)
5 lemons, halved
150 g (5½ oz) brown sugar
125 ml (4 fl oz/½ cup) red wine

Preheat the oven to 130°C (250°F/Gas 1).

Cut the necks, wing tips and leg knuckles off the ducks and reserve. Remove and reserve any organs from the cavities. Rinse the cavities out well, fill with the lemon halves, then rub all over with the sugar. Season to taste with sea salt and freshly ground black pepper.

Place the reserved duck pieces in a large flameproof roasting tray. Place the ducks on top and roast for 2½ hours. Remove from the oven and place the ducks on a wire rack placed over a tray to catch any juices. Discard the duck pieces.

Place the roasting tray over medium heat. Add the wine to the tray and deglaze, scraping the base with a wooden spoon to remove any cooked-on pieces. Add 375 ml (13 fl oz/1½ cups) water and simmer for 20 minutes. Strain through a fine sieve placed over a bowl. Return the sauce to the tray along with any resting juices from the ducks, place over low heat and simmer until reduced by half. Season to taste and serve with the ducks.

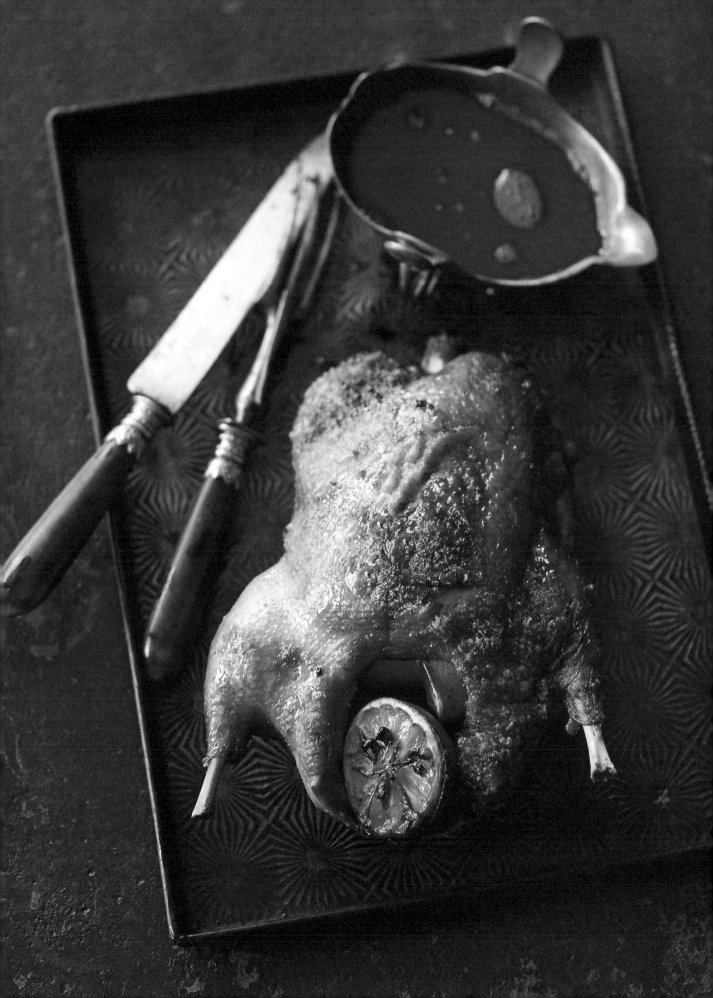

agnello farcito con spezie
lamb saddle filled with spice

serves 12

Rub the salt and pepper all over each half of the saddle and set aside for 20 minutes.

Place the herbs, green peppercorns, onion, chilli and garlic in a food processor and process until a smooth paste forms. Transfer to a bowl, then add the minced lamb, breadcrumbs and parmesan and combine well. Add the chopped egg, season to taste and combine well.

Working with one half of the saddle at a time, lay the lamb on a work surface. Place half of the mixture along the length of the lamb. Roll up tightly and secure at regular intervals with kitchen string.

Preheat the oven to 140°C (275°F/Gas 1).

Heat half of the oil in a large frying pan over high heat. Cook one piece of lamb until browned all over, then place on a wire rack in a large roasting tray. Repeat with the remaining oil and lamb. Roast for 2 hours for medium.

Remove from the oven, rest for 20 minutes, then untie the string, cut into slices and serve warm.

1½ tablespoons sea salt flakes
2 teaspoons coarsely ground black pepper
1 lamb saddle (about 2.5 kg/ 5 lb 8 oz), boned and halved lengthways (ask your butcher to do this)
1 bunch sage, leaves picked
2 tablespoons rosemary leaves
3 tablespoons drained green peppercorns in brine, crushed
2 brown onions, chopped
1 tablespoon confit red chilli (see page 263) or 1 long red chilli, seeds removed and chopped
8 garlic cloves or 8 confit garlic cloves (see page 263)
150 g (5½ oz) coarsely minced (ground) lamb (ask your butcher for a 60% meat to 40% fat ratio)
300 g (10½ oz/3¾ cups) fresh breadcrumbs
150 g (5½ oz/1½ cups) finely grated parmesan
4 eggs, hard-boiled, peeled and chopped
100 ml (3½ fl oz) olive oil

la griglia
sure-fire winners

This chapter about smoking and grilling is dedicated to my dad. He was a farmer who worked 18 hours a day on the land through wars, regional conflict, family woes and poverty. Despite all of this, he always put meat on the table for his family. He always used secondary cuts of meat; to get the most flavour from these cuts, he cooked them over a fire for a very long time over a low heat. Cooking in this way also saved wood.

Not having a stove was never an issue for my dad or other Italians because they just built one wherever they were. My dad once told me that slow cooking came about during the war. Cooking over flames created too much smoke so your enemies could easily find you, so they cooked their meat slowly over embers which didn't create as much smoke. It's a great story, although I'm not sure if it's true… but I believe him.

These are the recipes I cook with my dad every Sunday afternoon in the backyard on the barbecue, la griglia.

filetto con la peperonata
fillet steak with peperonata

serves 4

Slice the capsicums into finger-sized strips and place in a bowl.

Heat the oil in a heavy-based saucepan over medium–high heat until hot but not smoking. Add the basil, being careful as the oil will spit, and fry for 40 seconds or until translucent and crisp. Remove with a slotted spoon and drain on absorbent paper. Repeat with the parsley leaves, then the garlic.

Add the onion to the pan and cook over high heat for 5 minutes or until it begins to caramelise. Remove the pan from the heat, then gently stir in the capsicum, fried herbs and garlic. Season to taste with sea salt and freshly ground black pepper, toss gently to combine and stand until cooled to room temperature.

Place the cooled peperonata in a colander over a large shallow bowl to collect the juices.

Meanwhile, using the flat side of a meat mallet, bash out the steaks between baking paper until about 5 mm (¼ inch) thick all over. Place the steaks in the bowl with the peperonata juices and marinate for 3–4 minutes.

Preheat a barbecue flatplate or char-grill to high and lightly brush with oil. Remove the steaks from the marinade, allowing the excess to drain off, then season to taste. Cook for 30 seconds each side for medium-rare.

Squeeze the lemon halves over the steaks, then place on serving plates, place a large spoonful of peperonata on one half of each steak and fold over.

2 large red capsicums (peppers), roasted until skins blacken, peeled
2 large green capsicums (peppers), roasted until skins blacken, peeled
125 ml (4 fl oz/½ cup) olive oil, plus extra for brushing
10 basil leaves
¼ cup flat-leaf (Italian) parsley leaves
2 garlic cloves, thinly sliced
1 large brown onion, thinly sliced
4 fillet steaks (about 200 g/ 7 oz each)
2 lemons, halved

gamberoni all'aglio
grilled prawns with garlic butter

serves 4

80 g (2¾ oz) butter, softened
3 garlic cloves, chopped
1 tablespoon confit red chilli
   (see page 263) or
   1 long red chilli, seeds
   removed and chopped
2 tablespoons coarsely chopped
   flat-leaf (Italian) parsley
   leaves
juice of ½ lemon
16 large raw prawns (shrimp)
olive oil, for brushing

Place the butter, garlic, confit chilli, parsley and lemon juice in a food processor and season to taste with sea salt and freshly ground black pepper. Process until smooth and combined.

Using a sharp knife, butterfly the prawns. Cut down the back of the prawns, starting at the base of the head and finishing at the tail. Remove the veins and clean out the contents of the heads with a teaspoon — do not run the prawn heads under a tap as this will wash away the flavour. Open up the prawns and place, cut-side down, on a chopping board. Gently press down to flatten.

Preheat a barbecue flatplate to high and lightly brush with some oil. Cook the prawns, cut-side down, for 1 minute. Turn the prawns over and place a small spoonful of the butter mixture on top. Close the hood, turn off the burners and leave for 3 minutes. Enjoy hot straight from the barbecue.

pancetta affumicata
slow-smoked pork belly

serves 4

To make the green salt rub, place all of the ingredients in a food processor and process until a fragrant coarse green paste forms.

Rub the green salt all over the pork belly and skin, then shake off any excess. Place in a shallow dish and refrigerate for 1 hour.

Place half of the wood chips in a large bowl, cover with cold water and soak for 5 minutes.

Place three 50 cm (20 inch) long sheets of foil on top of each other. Drain the soaking wood chips and place in the centre of the foil along with the dry wood chips. Fold into a parcel, then prick holes in the top to allow smoke to escape.

Remove the char-grill plate from a barbecue. Place the wood-chip parcel directly onto the burner and turn onto low–medium heat (leave the other burners unlit). Allow the parcel to smoke for about 30 seconds, then remove with tongs, replace the grill plate and place the parcel on top.

Place the pork belly, skin-side up, on the cold half of the barbecue and close the hood. Cook for 2.5 hours, checking every hour or so, as the cooking time will vary depending on the type of barbecue used and the thickness of the pork belly. There is no need to turn the pork. When it is cooked, the meat should be incredibly tender and a fork should go through the fat very easily. The meat will have a fantastic aroma. Enjoy hot or cold the next day, shredded into a salad.

Note Wood chips are available from hardware stores and outdoor equipment shops.

750 g (1 lb 10 oz) piece of pork belly, skin on and scored
500 g (1 lb 2 oz) shaved wood chips, for smoking (see Note)

green salt rub
3 teaspoons sea salt flakes
1 teaspoon freshly ground black pepper
5 sage leaves
1½ tablespoons rosemary leaves
1 small handful flat-leaf (Italian) parsley leaves
2 garlic cloves

quaglie alla piastra
quail skewers

serves 4

1½ tablespoons olive oil,
    plus extra for brushing
1½ tablespoons red wine vinegar
1 tablespoon brown sugar
3 garlic cloves, finely chopped
16 sage leaves
8 butterflied quails (ask your
    butcher to do this)
8 thin metal or bamboo skewers
    (if using bamboo skewers,
    soak them in cold water
    for 30 minutes)
lemon wedges, to serve

Place the oil, vinegar, sugar and garlic in a bowl, season to taste with sea salt and freshly ground black pepper and whisk until the sugar is dissolved. Set aside.

Secure 2 sage leaves with toothpicks onto the flesh side of each quail. Thread 2 quails through the thighs and wings onto 2 parallel metal skewers. Repeat with the remaining quails and skewers.

Place the quails on a large tray and pour over the marinade. Cover and refrigerate for no longer than 15 minutes.

Meanwhile, preheat a barbecue flatplate or char-grill to medium–high and lightly brush with oil. Place the quails on the barbecue, skin-side down, close the hood and cook for 3 minutes, then turn, cover again and cook for another 3 minutes. Remove from the barbecue and rest for 4–5 minutes in a warm place before serving with the lemon wedges.

spiedini di pollo
chicken skewers

serves 4

Place the basil, parmesan, oil, pine nuts, garlic and pickled onions in a food processor and season to taste with sea salt and freshly ground black pepper. Process until a smooth pesto forms.

Thread a tenderloin onto each skewer and place in a large shallow container. Pour over the pesto and turn to coat well. Cover with plastic wrap and refrigerate overnight.

Preheat a barbecue flatplate or char-grill to high and lightly brush with oil. Cook the skewers for 3–4 minutes each side or until golden and just cooked through. Rest in a warm place for 5 minutes, then season to taste and serve hot.

8 basil leaves
20 g (¾ oz) finely grated
   parmesan
1½ tablespoons olive oil,
   plus extra for brushing
1 tablespoon pine nuts, toasted
1 large garlic clove
2 pickled onions
8 chicken tenderloins
8 thin metal or bamboo skewers
   (if using bamboo skewers,
   soak them in cold water
   for 30 minutes)

building a backyard grill

How to build a barbecue is something I learnt from my dad. It's an activitiy we do when our family celebrates new year or if we go hunting. Whenever we get together, in typical Italian style, everyone has an opinion about the right way to build a grill. Below is my way.

With the convenience of modern gas and charcoal barbecues, it may seem like a lot of effort to go to but the building of the grill becomes the purpose of the day and the eating at the end is the reward. The recipes in this chapter can easily be adapted to cooking on this type of makeshift barbecue. Use a large upturned metal bowl or roasting tray to cover the food, if required, making sure you use tongs to remove it when checking if your food is ready.

Equipment You'll need a shovel, eight or so bricks, a grill plate, a couple bags of charcoal, fire starters, some newspaper, a strong man and some sunshine.

Get your back into it Dig a hole about 50 cm (20 inches) long, wide and deep. Set the dirt aside, so you can refill the hole afterwards.

Solid foundation Lay down two bricks in the hole. Place the charcoal over the bricks, place some fire starters on top, then cover with scrunched-up newspaper.

All fired up Arrange the rest of the bricks to form a border around the hole. Light the newspaper and the fire starters should catch alight, then the charcoal.

Grill station Once the charcoal has died down to embers, place a char-grill plate or flatplate (you could even use a piece of clean chicken wire) on top of the bricks.

Buon appetito! Lightly brush the grill plate with oil and you're ready to start barbecuing.

costata di maiale arrosto
slow-roasted pork rack

serves 8

9-cutlet rack of pork (about
2.5 kg/5 lb 8 oz),
skin on and scored
1 quantity green salt rub
(see page 217)
⅓ cup lightly packed rosemary
sprigs
500 g (1 lb 2 oz) shaved
wood chips, for smoking
(see Note)

Rub the pork rack all over with the green salt rub, then shake off any excess. Using a small sharp knife, make small incisions in the fat and insert a small sprig of rosemary into each. Place the pork in the refrigerator until required.

Place half of the wood chips in a large bowl, cover with cold water and soak for 5 minutes.

Place three 50 cm (20 inch) long sheets of foil on top of each other. Drain the soaking wood chips and place in the centre of the foil along with the dry wood chips. Fold into a parcel, then prick holes in the top to allow smoke to escape.

Remove the char-grill plate from a barbecue. Place the wood chip parcel directly onto a burner and turn onto low–medium heat (leave the other burners unlit). Allow the parcel to smoke for about 30 seconds, then remove with tongs, replace the grill plate and place the parcel on top.

Place the pork rack, skin-side up, on the cold half of the barbecue and close the hood. Cook for 3 hours, checking every hour or so, as the cooking time will vary depending on the type of barbecue used. There is no need to turn the meat. When it is cooked, the meat should be juicy and tender and the skin golden and crisp. You can check for doneness using a meat thermometer. The internal temperature should be 70°C (150°F) for medium or 85°C (185°F) for very well done. Enjoy hot straight from the barbecue.

Note Wood chips are available from hardware stores and outdoor equipment shops.

cosce di pollo alla valdarnese
peppered chicken marylands

serves 4

500 g (1 lb 2 oz) wood chips,
    for smoking (see Note)
125 ml (4 fl oz/½ cup) white wine
1 tablespoon sea salt flakes
2 teaspoons freshly ground
    black pepper
4 chicken marylands
2 tablespoons olive oil

Place half of the wood chips in a large bowl, pour over the wine and stand for 5 minutes. Place three 50 cm (20 inch) long sheets of foil on top of each other. Drain the soaking wood chips and place in the centre of the foil along with the dry wood chips. Fold into a parcel, then prick holes in the top to allow smoke to escape.

Combine the salt and pepper together on a plate. Rub the marylands with the oil and lightly coat the skin in the salt and pepper mixture.

Remove the char-grill plate from a barbecue. Place the wood chip parcel directly onto a burner and turn onto low–medium heat (leave the other burners unlit). Allow the parcel to smoke for about 30 seconds, then remove with tongs, replace the grill plate and place the parcel on top.

Place the marylands, skin-side up, on the cold half of the barbecue and close the hood. Cook for 2 hours, checking every 20 minutes as the cooking time will vary depending on the type of barbecue used. When they are cooked, the skin should be golden and the juices should run clear when a skewer is inserted. Enjoy hot straight from the barbecue or cold the next day in a sandwich.

Note Wood chips are available from hardware stores and outdoor equipment shops.

filetto al salmoriglio
sicilian fillet steak

serves 4

Place the oil, oregano, parsley, garlic and lemon juice in a bowl. Season to taste with sea salt and freshly ground black pepper and combine well. It should taste quite lemony.

Preheat a barbecue flatplate or char-grill to high.

Using the flat side of a meat mallet, flatten the steaks between plastic wrap until 1.5 cm (⅝ inch) thick all over. Brush both sides of the steaks with a little dressing, then barbecue for 2 minutes each side for medium-rare or until cooked to your liking. Enjoy straight from the grill in an Italian bread roll with the remaining dressing drizzled over.

125 ml (4 fl oz/½ cup) extra virgin olive oil
1½ tablespoons coarsely chopped oregano leaves
1½ tablespoons coarsely chopped flat-leaf (Italian) parsley leaves
4 garlic cloves, finely chopped
juice of 2 small lemons
4 fillet steaks (about 200 g/7 oz each)
Italian bread rolls, to serve

girello di maiale
pork girello

serves 6

Rub the girello all over with the green salt rub, then shake off any excess.

Place the potato, carrot, pumpkin, garlic and shallots in a heavy-based roasting tray. Drizzle over the oil, season to taste with sea salt and freshly ground black pepper and toss to coat well.

Preheat a barbecue flatplate to high and lightly brush with oil. Cook the girello until browned all over, then place on top of the vegetables. Place the tray on the hot flatplate and when the tray is hot, add the wine, then close the hood. Reduce the heat to medium and cook for 2–3 hours, checking every 30 minutes, as the cooking time will vary depending on the type of barbecue used. When it is cooked, the juices should run clear when a skewer is inserted. You can check for doneness using a meat thermometer. The internal temperature should be 68°C (155°F).

Note Girello is one of the muscles that make up the silverside. It is my favourite cut for slow roasting. If it is cooked fast, it will be tough and chewy. It can be ordered through a good Italian butcher.

1 whole pork girello (about 1.2 kg/2 lb 10 oz) (see Note)
1 quantity green salt rub (see page 217)
3 large kipfler potatoes, quartered
3 carrots, cut into 6 cm (2½ inch) lengths
½ jap pumpkin, unpeeled and cut into wedges
12 garlic cloves
12 French shallots
60 ml (2 fl oz/¼ cup) olive oil, plus extra for brushing
125 ml (4 fl oz/½ cup) white wine

galletto all'arrabbiata
spatchcock with tomato & chilli

serves 4

4 butterflied spatchcocks
80 ml (2½ fl oz/⅓ cup) olive oil
2 garlic cloves, sliced
1 tablespoon confit red chilli (see page 263) or 1 long red chilli, seeds removed and chopped
5 ox heart tomatoes, peeled and diced
2 tablespoons chopped flat-leaf (Italian) parsley

Preheat a barbecue to high with the hood closed.

Rub the spatchcocks all over with half of the oil and season to taste with sea salt and freshly ground black pepper.

Reduce the barbecue heat to medium–high. Place a large heavy-based roasting tray on top of the char-grill plate, add the remaining oil, garlic, chilli and tomato and cook, stirring regularly, for 15 minutes or until the tomato has broken down and a thick sauce has formed. Stir in the parsley.

Meanwhile, cook the spatchcock, skin-side down first, on the flatplate until browned on both sides. Place the spatchcock, skin-side up, in the sauce in the roasting tray. Close the hood and cook for 20–25 minutes or until the spatchcock is tender, checking after 15 minutes as the cooking time will vary depending on the type of barbecue used. Enjoy hot or cold. Any leftovers will make a great sauce for pasta — simply shred any meat into the sauce ready to stir through hot pasta the next day.

tonno lessato al burro
butter-poached tuna cannon

serves 4

Place the sage and confit chilli in a small food processor and process until finely chopped. Set aside.

Preheat a barbecue flatplate to low-medium.

Place the butter, mineral water and green chillies in a small deep cast-iron casserole. Place on the flatplate, close the hood and bring to a simmer.

Rub the sage mixture onto the tuna, lightly brush with some oil and season to taste with sea salt and freshly ground black pepper. Add any remaining sage mixture to the casserole.

Sear the tuna on the flatplate for 1 minute on all sides, then place in the casserole. Reduce the heat to as low as possible so that the poaching liquid is just below a simmer. Poach the tuna for 20 minutes for medium-rare, basting the tuna regularly with the liquid and turning so it cooks evenly. Remove the tuna from the casserole and allow to cool to room temperature. Keep the poaching liquid warm.

To serve, using a very sharp knife, thinly slice the tuna and arrange on plates. Spoon over some of the warm poaching liquid, season to taste and drizzle over the extra virgin olive oil.

16 sage leaves
1 tablespoon confit green chilli
  (see page 263)
500 g (1 lb 2 oz) unsalted butter
250 ml (9 fl oz/1 cup) sparkling
  mineral water
5 small green chillies
400 g (14 oz) cannon of tuna
  (ask your fishmonger for this)
olive oil, for brushing
extra virgin olive oil, for drizzling

dentice in acqua pazza
whole snapper in crazy water

serves 4

80 ml (2½ fl oz/⅓ cup) olive oil

4 whole plate-sized snappers
   (about 400–450 g/14 oz–1 lb
   each), fins and tails trimmed,
   flesh scored

450 g (1 lb) desiree potatoes
   (about 2 large), peeled
   and cut into 1.5 cm (⅝ inch)
   cubes

8 French shallots, thinly sliced

60 ml (2 fl oz/¼ cup) white wine

½ bunch flat-leaf (Italian)
   parsley, leaves picked
   and chopped

250 ml (9 fl oz/1 cup) sparkling
   mineral water

6 marinated artichoke hearts
   in oil, drained and quartered

60 ml (2 fl oz/¼ cup) extra virgin
   olive oil

1 head radicchio, outer leaves
   discarded, leaves separated

75 g (2¾ oz) butter, chopped

Place a large heavy-based flameproof baking dish on a barbecue flatplate, turn the burners on high and close the hood.

When the barbecue is hot, heat half of the olive oil in the baking dish. Add 2 of the snappers to the dish and cook for 3 minutes each side or until just golden, then remove and set aside. Repeat with the remaining snappers.

Add the remaining olive oil to the dish and when hot, add the potato and shallot and cook, stirring frequently, for 10 minutes or until lightly coloured. Pour in the wine and simmer for 1–2 minutes or until reduced by half. Place the snappers on top, reduce the temperature to medium–high, then add the parsley and mineral water. Close the hood and simmer for 11–12 minutes or until the fish is just cooked through. Remove the snappers from the dish and place on a large platter.

Add the artichokes, extra virgin olive oil and radicchio leaves to the dish. Once the leaves begin to wilt, add the butter and season to taste with sea salt and freshly ground black pepper. Pour the 'acqua pazza' over the snappers and enjoy hot.

dolci
sweet somethings

Pastry is not my strongest point, so I like to keep things simple and traditional. These recipes are the ones handed down to me from my family. I have them on my restaurant menu nearly all the time. They are simple in flavours but absolutely irresistible. (My customers find it hard to say no!) Typically in an Italian home, when it is time for sweets, everything — cakes, small things to nibble — comes out at once and is left on the table for grazing. Once coffee and crostoli have been served at the end of the meal, it means 'good night'. The crostoli are one last bite, a sweet 'thank you' to your guests for their company.

panna cotta

makes 4

Place the milk, cream, sugar and vanilla bean seeds in a small saucepan. Bring to a simmer, then remove from the heat.

Soak the gelatine in cold water until softened. Drain and squeeze out any excess water. Stir the gelatine into the hot cream mixture until smooth. Pour into a jug and stand until lukewarm. Stir the mixture to distribute the vanilla bean seeds evenly, then pour into four 125 ml (4 fl oz/½ cup) capacity dariole moulds and refrigerate overnight.

To serve, remove the panna cottas from the refrigerator 30 minutes before serving. Combine the strawberries and enough red wine to moisten and chill until ready to serve. When the panna cottas are at room temperature, loosen the edges with your fingers, then invert onto plates and serve with the strawberries in wine.

250 ml (9 fl oz/1 cup) milk
250 ml (9 fl oz/1 cup) pouring (single) cream
125 g (4½ oz) caster (superfine) sugar
½ vanilla bean, halved and seeds scraped
1½ gelatine leaves, titanium strength
sliced strawberries in red wine, to serve

torta di formaggio
cheesecake

makes 6

250 g (9 oz/1 cup) cream cheese,
    at room temperature
190 ml (6½ fl oz) sweetened
    condensed milk
100 ml (3½ fl oz) pouring
    (single) cream
zest of 1 lemon
1 tablespoon lemon juice
amaretti or pasta mandorla
    (soft almond biscuits),
    lightly crushed

Place the cream cheese in the bowl of an electric mixer and beat until light and fluffy. With the motor still running, slowly add the condensed milk and beat until smooth.

Whisk the cream in a separate bowl until soft peaks form. Fold the cream into the cream cheese mixture until just combined. Fold in the lemon zest and juice. Place some amaretti in the bases of six 125 ml (4 fl oz/½ cup) capacity glasses, then pour in the cream cheese mixture. Refrigerate for 4 hours or until set.

Scatter amaretti over each cheesecake to serve.

bignè al cioccolato
chocolate puffs

serves 6

melted chocolate, to serve

chocolate custard
150 g (5½ oz) dark chocolate,
    chopped
12 egg yolks
150 g (5½ oz) caster (superfine)
    sugar
90 g (3¼ oz/¾ cup) cornflour
    (cornstarch)
200 ml (7 fl oz) pouring
    (single) cream
400 ml (14 fl oz) milk

puffs
50 g (1¾ oz) unsalted butter
60 g (2¼ oz) plain (all-purpose)
    flour
2 eggs

chocolate cream
150 g (5½ oz) dark chocolate,
    chopped
4 egg yolks
400 ml (14 fl oz) pouring
    (single) cream

To make the chocolate custard, place the chocolate in a heatproof bowl over a saucepan of just-simmering water and stir until melted and smooth. Remove from the heat and cool. Place the egg yolks and sugar in the bowl of an electric mixer and beat until thick and pale. Stir in the cornflour, then add the melted chocolate and combine well. Set aside. Place the cream and milk in a saucepan over medium heat and bring to a simmer. Stirring continuously with a wooden spoon, gradually add to the chocolate mixture. Combine well, then return the mixture to the pan and place over low heat. Stir until the custard thickens enough to just coat the back of a wooden spoon. Remove from the heat, pour into a bowl and cover closely with plastic wrap to prevent a skin forming. Cool, then refrigerate overnight.

To make the puffs, preheat the oven to 180°C (350°F/Gas 4). Place the butter, 150 ml (5 fl oz) water and a pinch of salt in a heavy-based saucepan over medium heat and bring to the boil. Add the flour and beat vigorously for 1–2 minutes or until the dough comes away from the sides of the pan. Remove from the heat, add the eggs, one at a time, beating well after each addition. Return to low heat and continue to beat for 2–3 minutes or until silky and smooth. Transfer the dough to a piping bag fitted with a 1 cm (½ inch) plain nozzle. Pipe golf-ball-sized rounds onto baking trays lined with baking paper, at least 5 cm (2 inches) apart. Bake for 20 minutes or until golden and puffed. Place on a wire rack until completely cooled, then store in an airtight container for up to 5 days.

To make the chocolate cream, place the chocolate in a heatproof bowl over a saucepan of just-simmering water and stir until melted and smooth. Remove from the heat and while still hot, add the egg yolks and combine well. Whisk the cream until soft peaks form, then fold in the chocolate mixture and stand at room temperature until needed.

To fill the puffs, make a small hole in the base of each puff. Spoon the custard into a piping bag fitted with a 1 cm (½ inch) plain nozzle, then pipe it into the puffs. Roll the puffs in the chocolate cream, drizzle over the melted chocolate, serve and indulge. These are best eaten on the day of filling.

zuppa inglese
italian trifle

makes 6

200 g (7 oz) fresh berries, to serve

vanilla custard
6 egg yolks
75 g (2¾ oz) caster (superfine)
    sugar
45 g (1¾ oz) cornflour
    (cornstarch)
100 ml (3½ fl oz) pouring
    (single) cream
200 ml (7 fl oz) milk
½ teaspoon vanilla extract

berry jelly
2 gelatine leaves, titanium
    strength
150 ml (5 fl oz) strained berry
    juice (see Note)
50 g (1¾ oz) caster (superfine)
    sugar

sponge
3 eggs, separated
a large pinch of cream of tartar
180 g (6½ oz) caster (superfine)
    sugar
110 g (3¾ oz) unsalted butter,
    softened
140 g (5 oz) plain (all-purpose)
    flour
½ teaspoon baking powder

To make the vanilla custard, place the egg yolks and sugar in the bowl of an electric mixer and beat until thick and pale. Stir in the cornflour and combine well. Set aside. Place the cream and milk in a saucepan over medium heat and bring to a simmer. While whisking continuously, gradually add the hot cream to the egg yolk mixture. Combine well, then return to the pan and place over low heat. Stir until the custard thickens enough to coat the back of a wooden spoon well. Remove from the heat, stir in the vanilla extract, then pour into a bowl and cover closely with plastic wrap to prevent a skin forming. Cool, then refrigerate overnight.

Meanwhile, to make the berry jelly, soak the gelatine leaves in cold water until softened. Place the berry juice, sugar and 150 ml (5 fl oz) water in a small saucepan and bring to a simmer, stirring to make sure the sugar is dissolved. Drain the gelatine, squeeze out the excess water, then add to the pan and stir until dissolved. Strain through a fine sieve and pour into a 500 ml (17 fl oz/2 cup) capacity shallow dish. Cool, then refrigerate overnight or until set.

To make the sponge, preheat the oven to 180°C (350°F/Gas 4). Lightly grease a lamington tin. Whisk the egg white and cream of tartar until soft peaks form. Gradually add half of the sugar and whisk until thick and glossy. Set aside. Place the butter and the remaining sugar in the bowl of an electric mixer and beat until light and fluffy. Add the egg yolks and beat until well combined. Sift over the flour, baking powder and a large pinch of salt and fold in gently. Fold in the egg white, then pour into the prepared pan. Bake for 50–60 minutes or until an inserted skewer comes out clean. Turn out onto a wire rack and cool completely.

To assemble the trifle, cut the jelly and sponge into 1 cm (½ inch) cubes. Divide one-quarter of the custard among six 300 ml (10½ fl oz) capacity glasses. Top with one-third of the sponge, then one-third of the jelly. Repeat to make 2 more layers and finish with a layer of custard. Top with the berries and refrigerate until serving.

Note You will need about 200 g (7 oz) berries for this amount of juice. Blend the berries in a blender, then pass through a fine sieve, discarding the solids.

budino alla vaniglia
burnt vanilla creams

makes 6

8 egg yolks
220 g (7¾ oz/1 cup) caster
   (superfine) sugar
30 g (1 oz/¼ cup) cornflour
   (cornstarch)
500 ml (17 fl oz/2 cups) pouring
   (single) cream
½ vanilla bean, halved and seeds
   scraped

Place the egg yolks, half of the sugar and all of the cornflour in the bowl of an electric mixer and beat until thick and pale.

Place the cream and vanilla bean seeds in a small saucepan over low heat and stir until just before the cream comes to a simmer. Stirring continuously with a wooden spoon, gradually add the hot cream to the egg yolk mixture until well combined. Return the mixture to the pan over low heat and stir until the mixture thickens enough to coat the back of a wooden spoon. Do not allow it to come to the boil.

Pour the mixture into six 150 ml (5½ fl oz) capacity ramekins. Cool, then refrigerate for at least 4 hours or until set.

Remove the creams from the refrigerator 20 minutes before serving and bring to room temperature. Just before serving, sprinkle the tops evenly with the remaining sugar. Using a kitchen blowtorch, melt the sugar until dark golden. Stand for a few minutes before serving.

tiramisù

serves 8

Place the egg yolks and sugar in the bowl of
an electric mixer and beat until thick and pale.

In a separate bowl, whisk the cream until
soft peaks form. Fold in the egg yolk mixture until
a smooth mousse forms.

Combine the coffee and Frangelico in a
shallow bowl.

Spread 250 ml (9 fl oz/1 cup) of the mousse over
the base of a shallow 1.5 litre (52 fl oz) capacity
glass bowl. Working with one at a time, dip the
savoiardi biscuits briefly into the coffee mixture,
then arrange in a single layer on top of the mousse.
Repeat with the remaining mousse, biscuits and
coffee mixture, finishing with a layer of mousse.
There should be no biscuits showing on the top.
Refrigerate for at least 4 hours.

Dust generously with cocoa to serve.

10 egg yolks

70 g (2½ oz) caster (superfine)
sugar

200 ml (7 fl oz) pouring
(single) cream

300 ml (10½ fl oz) freshly made
espresso coffee

100 ml (3½ fl oz) Frangelico

20 savoiardi (sponge finger)
biscuits

cocoa, for dusting

babà
rum baba

makes 12

50 ml (1¾ fl oz) milk
10 g (¼ oz) fresh yeast
    (see Note page 62)
10 g (¼ oz) caster (superfine)
    sugar
250 g (9 oz/1⅔ cups) plain
    (all-purpose) flour,
    plus extra for dusting
4 eggs, lightly beaten
zest of ½ lemon
125 g (4½ oz) unsalted butter,
    diced and softened

rum syrup
250 g (9 oz) caster (superfine)
    sugar
100 ml (3½ fl oz) good-quality rum

Heat the milk in a small saucepan until 30°C (86°F) or lukewarm. Add the yeast and sugar and stir until dissolved.

Place the flour and 1 teaspoon salt in the bowl of an electric mixer fitted with a dough hook and make a well in the centre. Add the yeast mixture, beaten egg and lemon zest to the well. With the motor on low speed, mix until just combined. Turn out onto a lightly floured surface and knead for 10–12 minutes or until smooth and elastic. Place the dough in a lightly greased bowl, cover with a tea towel and stand in a warm place for 20 minutes or until risen by half.

Punch down the dough with your fist, then return it to the mixer. With the motor on low speed, gradually add the butter, one piece at a time, until the mixture is smooth and glossy. Return to the lightly oiled bowl, cover and stand in a warm place for another 30 minutes or until risen by half again.

Punch the dough down with your fist and divide into 12 pieces. Shape each into a ball and place, seam-side down, into lightly greased 80 ml (2½ fl oz/ ⅓ cup) capacity baba tins or dariole moulds. Place on a baking tray, cover with a tea towel and stand for 20 minutes or until risen by three-quarters.

Preheat the oven to 190°C (375°F/Gas 5). Bake the babas for 30 minutes or until golden and risen. Remove from the oven, stand in the tins for 5 minutes, then turn out onto a wire rack to cool.

Meanwhile, to make the rum syrup, place the sugar, rum and 150 ml (5 fl oz) water in a large saucepan over low heat and stir until the sugar is dissolved. Simmer for 10 minutes. Remove from the heat, then add the cooled babas and stand for 4–5 minutes or until they are well soaked. Serve the babas with the rum syrup spooned over.

These biscuits are also called 'chiacchiere' which means chatter.
It's the sound they make when you bite into one of these crunchy crisp
pastries and they're usually eaten over coffee chatting with friends.

crostoli
fried pastry

makes about 40

Place the butter and caster sugar in the bowl of an electric mixer and beat until light and fluffy. Add the egg yolks, grappa and vanilla bean seeds and beat until creamy and smooth. Add the flour and stir until the dough comes together. Divide dough into 2, shape into discs, wrap in plastic wrap and refrigerate for 2 hours.

Roll out the dough between baking paper until about 2 mm (¹⁄₁₆ inch) thick or as thin as possible. Cut into 8 x 4 cm (3¼ x 1½ inch) strips. (You can freeze the cut, uncooked crostoli at this stage. Place on a baking tray lined with baking paper in a single layer, then wrap in plastic wrap and freeze for up to 6 weeks. (There is no need to defrost, you can deep-fry them frozen.)

Heat the oil in a deep-fryer or large deep saucepan to 160°C (315°F) or until a cube of bread dropped into the oil browns in 30 seconds. Deep-fry the crostoli, in batches, until golden on both sides. Remove with tongs and drain on absorbent paper. While still hot, dust with the icing sugar.

Once completely cooled, crostoli will keep, in an airtight container, for up to 3 days.

40 g (1½ oz) unsalted butter, chopped and softened
60 g (2¼ oz) caster (superfine) sugar
2 egg yolks
30 ml (1 fl oz) grappa
½ vanilla bean, halved and seeds scraped
275 g (9¾ oz) plain (all-purpose) flour, sifted
olive oil, for deep-frying
icing (confectioner's) sugar, for dusting

cannoli di ricotta
ricotta cannoli

makes about 15

1 quantity crostoli pastry
   (see page 255)
500 ml (17 fl oz/2 cups) olive oil,
   for deep-frying, plus extra
   for oiling
1 egg white, lightly beaten
icing (confectioner's) sugar,
   for dusting

ricotta cream
300 g (10½ oz) fresh ricotta
45 g (1¾ oz) caster (superfine)
   sugar
60 g (2¼ oz) mixed candied fruit,
   finely chopped
60 g (2¼ oz) dark chocolate
   buttons, finely chopped
cannoli tubes (see Note)

Roll out the crostoli pastry between baking paper until 2 mm (¹⁄₁₆ inch) thick. Cut into 4 cm (1½ inch) squares.

Lightly oil the cannoli tubes with the extra oil. Wrap a pastry square diagonally around each tube. Secure the overlapping corners with the beaten egg white and press the corners firmly together.

Heat the oil in a deep-fryer or large deep saucepan to 160°C (315°F) or until a cube of bread dropped into the oil browns in 30 seconds. Deep-fry the cannoli, in batches, until golden and crisp all over. Remove using tongs and drain on absorbent paper. As soon as the tubes are cool enough to handle, slide them out and leave the pastries on a wire rack to cool completely.

To make the ricotta cream, place the ricotta and caster sugar in the bowl of an electric mixer and beat until smooth and the sugar is dissolved. Add the candied fruit and chocolate and combine well.

Fill a piping bag fitted with a small plain nozzle with the ricotta filling. Pipe the mixture into each end of the cannoli shells. Dust with the icing sugar and serve with an espresso.

Note Cannoli tubes are available from kitchen homeware stores and specialist baking shops.